TerraNova
SUCCESS STRATEGIES
Grade 8

**TerraNova Test Review
for the
TerraNova, Third Edition**

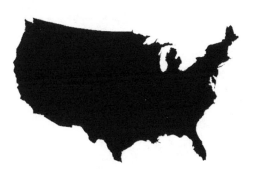

Dear Future Exam Success Story:

Congratulations on your purchase of our study guide. Our goal in writing our study guide was to cover the content on the test, as well as provide insight into typical test taking mistakes and how to overcome them.

Standardized tests are a key component of being successful, which only increases the importance of doing well in the high-pressure high-stakes environment of test day. How well you do on this test will have a significant impact on your future, and we have the research and practical advice to help you execute on test day.

The product you're reading now is designed to exploit weaknesses in the test itself, and help you avoid the most common errors test takers frequently make.

How to use this study guide

We don't want to waste your time. Our study guide is fast-paced and fluff-free. We suggest going through it a number of times, as repetition is an important part of learning new information and concepts.

First, read through the study guide completely to get a feel for the content and organization. Read the general success strategies first, and then proceed to the content sections. Each tip has been carefully selected for its effectiveness.

Second, read through the study guide again, and take notes in the margins and highlight those sections where you may have a particular weakness.

Finally, bring the manual with you on test day and study it before the exam begins.

Your success is our success

We would be delighted to hear about your success. Send us an email and tell us your story. Thanks for your business and we wish you continued success.

Sincerely,

Mometrix Test Preparation Team

Need more help? Check out our flashcards at:
http://MometrixFlashcards.com/terranova

TABLE OF CONTENTS

Top 15 Test Taking Tips

1. Know the test directions, duration, topics, question types, how many questions
2. Setup a flexible study schedule at least 3-4 weeks before test day
3. Study during the time of day you are most alert, relaxed, and stress free
4. Maximize your learning style; visual learner use visual study aids, auditory learner use auditory study aids
5. Focus on your weakest knowledge base
6. Find a study partner to review with and help clarify questions
7. Practice, practice, practice
8. Get a good night's sleep; don't try to cram the night before the test
9. Eat a well balanced meal
10. Wear comfortable, loose fitting, layered clothing; prepare for it to be either cold or hot during the test
11. Eliminate the obviously wrong answer choices, then guess the first remaining choice
12. Pace yourself; don't rush, but keep working and move on if you get stuck
13. Maintain a positive attitude even if the test is going poorly
14. Keep your first answer unless you are positive it is wrong
15. Check your work, don't make a careless mistake

Mathematics

Converting a decimal with a repeating pattern into a rational number

To convert a decimal with a repeating pattern into a rational number, write the equation x = decimal number. Then multiply each side of the equation by 10n, where n is the number of repeating digits. Subtract the first equation from the second equation, and solve the resulting equation for x.

Example:

$$x = 0.207207207\ldots$$
$$1000x = 207.207207207\ldots$$
$$999x = 207$$
$$x = \frac{207}{999} = \frac{23}{111}$$

Show how to determine the approximate location of an irrational number $\sqrt{n}$ on the number line, where 0 < n < 100, without a calculator. Include an example.

To find the approximate location of $\sqrt{n}$ on the number line, find consecutive integers a and b such that a2 < n < b2. This means that a < $\sqrt{n}$ < b and the irrational number lies between a and b on the number line. If n is closer to a2 than it is to b2, place $\sqrt{n}$ a little closer to a than b.

Example:

$$\sqrt{51}$$
$$7^2 = 49, 8^2 = 64$$
$$\sqrt{49} < \sqrt{51} < \sqrt{64}$$
$$7 < \sqrt{51} < 8$$

Place $\sqrt{51}$ closer to 7 than 8, because 49 is closer to 51 than 64:

Writing the properties of integer exponents for simplifying expressions of the form $a^m a^n, \frac{a^m}{a^n}$, and $(a^m)^n$

The properties of integer exponents for simplifying expressions of the form $a^m a^n, \frac{a^m}{a^n}$, and $(a^m)^n$ are as follows:

$$a^m a^n = a^{m+n}$$
$$\frac{a^m}{a^n} = a^{m-n}$$
$$(a^m)^n = a^{mn}$$

The only restriction on the value of a is that $a \neq 0$ for $\frac{a^m}{a^n}$.

Perfect square and perfect cube

The term perfect square means a number that is equal to the square of an integer. This means that the square root of the perfect square is itself an integer. For example, 16 is a perfect square because $4^2 = 16$, and $\sqrt{16} = 4$. A perfect cube is a number that is a cube of an integer. The number 8 is a perfect cube, because $2^3 = 8$, and correspondingly $\sqrt[3]{8} = 2$. If a number is not a perfect square, then the square root of the number is irrational. Similarly, a number that is not a perfect cube has a cube root that is irrational.

Scientific notation

A number is written in scientific notation when it has the form $a \times 10^n$, where $1 \leq a < 10$ and n is an integer. A very small number such as 0.0000000032 can be written in scientific notation by counting the number of places the decimal point must move to the right before the value of the number is at least 1. In this example, moving the decimal point 9 places gives the value 3.2. If a = 3.2, then the exponent n must be –9 to make up for multiplying by 10^9:

$0.0000000032 = 3.2 \times 10^{-9}$.

Notation 1E8

The notation 1E8 displayed on a calculator is in scientific notation. This is a shorthand notation that the calculator uses, so that it can fit very large and very small numbers on the screen. The letter E stands for exponent, and the number that follows the E is the value of the exponent on the number 10. The number before the E is multiplied by the power of 10 indicated. The expression 1E8 has the value 1×10^8, or 100,000,000. Note that because the number is in scientific notation, the number before the E is always at least 1 and less than 10.

Proportion

A proportion is an equation that has a ratio on each side of the equal sign. The ratios may be in the form of a fraction, such as $\frac{x}{100}$, or written with a colon, such as 3:5. For example, suppose two classes have 3 girls for every 2 boys. The ratio of girls to boys is 3:2.

To find the number of boys in a class with 25 students, write a proportion:

$$\frac{\text{number of boys}}{\text{number of students}} = \frac{2}{5} = \frac{x}{25}$$

In this proportion, the ratios represent the number of boys: number of students.

Determining the slope-intercept form of an equation for a non-vertical line

The slope-intercept form of a line is $y = mx + b$, where m is the slope of the line and b is the y-intercept. The slope of the line can be determined using the formula $m = \frac{y_1 - y_0}{x_1 - x_0}$, where (x_0, y_0) and (x_1, y_1) are two distinct points on the graph of the line. To find the value of b if not known from the graph, solve the equation $y_1 = mx_1 + b$ after substituting the values for m, x_1, and y_1. Finally, write the slope-intercept form of the line $y = mx + b$ with the values of m and b substituted into the equation.

Solving a linear equation in one variable

When solving a linear equation in one variable, if the process results in a true equation of the form $a = a$ where a is a real number, the equation has infinitely many solutions. This is because the equation is always true, independent of the value of the variable. For example, consider the solution of the equation below:

$$2x - 3(x + 1) = 2 - (x + 5)$$
$$2x - 3x - 3 = 2 - x - 5$$
$$-x - 3 = -x - 3$$
$$-3 = -3$$

For any value of x, each side of the equation evaluates to 3. So the solution is $x =$ any real number, and there are infinitely many solutions.

Coefficient and like terms

It is often necessary to add or subtract terms when solving a linear equation. Like terms are terms that have the same variable part. For example, $4x$ and $-2x$ are like terms, or x terms. Similarly, $\frac{3}{4}$ and $0.2x$ are like terms. The coefficients of these terms are the real numbers that multiply the variable part. To collect like terms, add the coefficients and keep the same variable part.

$$4x + (-2x) = (4 - 2)x = 2x$$

$$\frac{3x}{4} + 0.2x = \frac{3x}{4} + \frac{x}{5} = \frac{19x}{20}$$

Different possibilities that can occur graphically for a given system of two linear equations in two variables

There are 3 possibilities that can occur graphically for a given system of two linear equations in two variables:
1. The graphs intersect. The point at which they intersect is the solution of the system of equations.
2. The graphs are the same, or coincide with each other. This means that the two equations are actually the same equation. The solution of the system is all points on the line.
3. The graphs do not intersect, and the system has no solution. This occurs when the two equations have the same slope, or the two lines are distinct vertical lines. These lines are parallel.

Substitution method for solving a linear system of equations in two variables

The substitution method for solving a linear system of equations in two variables involves solving one equation for a particular variable. Then, the expression for that variable is substituted into the other equation, resulting in a one-variable equation that can be solved.

To determine the value of the other variable, substitute the value of the solved variable into one of the original equations. Example:

$x - 2y = -3$

$2x + y = -1$ Solve the second equation for y: $y = -2x - 1$

Substitute into the 1st equation:

$x - 2(-2x - 1) = -3$

$5x + 2 = -3$

$x = -1$

Substitute into the first equation:

$(-1) - 2y = -3$

$-2y = -2$

$y = 1$

The solution of the system is $(-1, 1)$.

Determining the values of a and b, when the sum and the difference of two numbers a and b are both 15, with $a > b$

The values of a and b can be determined by setting up and solving a system of linear equations in two variables. Suppose the sum of the variables is 15, and the difference is 15. Then a plus b equals 15, and a minus b equals 15. Note that $b - a$ will not work, because $a > b$, and this difference would result in a negative number. Write the system as follows:

$a + b = 15$

$a - b = 15$

Since $a > b$, write the difference as $a - b$.

Solve the system to find that $a = 15$ and $b = 0$.

Functions and relations

Functions and relations are alike in that both are sets of ordered pairs wherein each pair is an input (the first value) and an associated output (the second value). Functions and relations are different in that a function has only one output (a "unique" output) for each input, but a relation may have more than one output for each input (the output is not necessarily unique). Consequently, functions are relations, but relations are not necessarily functions. The following sets are examples of a relation that is not a function, and a function:

- relation (not a function): $\{(1, 4), (2, 3), (3, 4), (1, 2)\}$
- function: $\{(1, 4), (2, 3), (3, 4), (4, 0)\}$

The input 1 has two different outputs (4 and 2) in the relation, so it is not a function.

Determining the rate of change for a linear function using a table of values for the function

The rate of change can be determined for a linear function using a table of values by calculating the change in the dependent variable divided by the change in the independent variable for two data points. The points can be any two points from the table. This value is also equal to the slope of the graph of the linear function. Care should be taken to calculate the change in each variable in the same direction, so that an error in the sign of the rate of change is not made. For example, if two data points from the table are $(3, 6)$ and $(5, 1)$, then the rate of change is $6 - 1 = 5$ divided by $3 - 5 = -2$, or -2.5.

Recognizing a linear function from its graph

A linear function can be recognized from its graph by noting that all of the points of the graph fall on a straight line. This means that a line drawn with a straightedge through any two points of the graph will coincide with the entire graph of the function. One exception, however, is a vertical line. Although it is straight, it is not a linear function because it is not a function. A function has a unique output value for each input value, but a vertical line has every real number as an output value for one input value.

For a linear function that models the cost to rent a canoe for a certain number of hours, the rate of change indicates the cost per hour to rent the canoe. This is because the rate of change is the change in the dependent variable, or the cost, divided by the change in the independent variable, or the number of hours. The initial value of the function gives the cost to rent the canoe for the least allowed number of hours. For example, the point (0, 0) might represent the initial value or cost of $0 for renting the canoe for 0 hours. However, if a minimum 2-hour rental was required, the initial value would be 2 times the rate of change, and the point would have an x-coordinate of 2.

Determing when the function is increasing, decreasing, and has a minimum value for the function $y = x^2$

The graph of the function $y = x^2$ is a parabola. It takes on a minimum value of 0 at $x = 0$, which is the vertex of the parabola at (0, 0). For all negative values of x, the function is decreasing. This is because the graph falls from left to right. The graph starts to flatten out as x approaches 0. Then for all positive values of x, the function is increasing. This is because the graph rises from left to right. The further away from $x = 0$ the x-value of the function is, the greater the rate at which the function decreases or increases at that point of the function. This is evident from the steepness of the graph.

Effect of reflecting a vertical line segment in the third quadrant over the y-axis

When a vertical segment in the third quadrant is reflected over the y-axis, the reflected image is in the fourth quadrant. The image will be the same distance from the y-axis. Specifically, the x-coordinates of the image will be the opposites of the x-coordinates of the original segment, and the y-coordinates will be the same as the original segment. The length of the segment will be the same as the original segment. This is because reflections in the coordinate plane result in images that are congruent to the original figure.

An equilateral triangle is rotated clockwise 90° about the origin, determe how this will affect the measures of the angles of the triangle

A rotation clockwise of 90° about the origin will not affect the measures of the angles of the triangle. This is because for any rotation in the coordinate plane, angles are taken to angles of the same measure. In fact, the image triangle will also be an equilateral triangle, with 60° angle measures, that is congruent to the original triangle. The only angles that change are the angles related to the position of the triangle relative to the origin. Specifically, the segments from the origin to the vertices of the original triangle have rotated 90° clockwise, with the endpoint at the origin remaining fixed.

Translation of a line in the coordinate plane results in a line parallel to the original line

Suppose two points on the original line are (a, b) and (c, d). This means the slope of the line is $\frac{d-b}{c-a}$, or for $a = c$ the line is a vertical line. Translate the line m units vertically and n units horizontally. The points (a, b) and (c, d) are now at $(a + m, b + n)$ and $(c + m, d + n)$. The slope of this line is $\frac{d+n-b-n}{c+m-a-m} = \frac{d-b}{c-a}$, which is the same as the original line, or a vertical line for $a = c$. This means the line is parallel to the original line.

Transformations can be used to prove two figures in the coordinate plane are congruent

Two figures in the coordinate plane can be proven congruent by showing there is a sequence of transformations that obtains one figure from the other. The transformations can include rotations, reflections, or translations. For each point on the original figure, the sequence of transformations takes that point to the corresponding point of the second figure. For example, if triangle ABC is congruent to triangle FGH, then the sequence of transformations takes vertex A to vertex F, vertex B to vertex G, and vertex C to vertex H. It also takes each point on every side of triangle ABC to each point on every side of triangle FGH.

A square in the coordinate plane is dilated by a factor of 2. How this will affect the coordinates of the vertices of the square and the area of the square?

If a square in the coordinate plane is dilated by a factor of 2, the coordinates of the vertices of the square will all be multiplied by 2. For example, if $(3, 0)$ was a vertex point of the square, the dilation takes this point to $(6, 0)$. The area of the square will be multiplied by a factor of 4. This can be illustrated by considering a square with vertices at $(0, 0)$, $(0, a)$, (a, a), and $(a, 0)$. These points become $(0, 0)$, $(0, 2a)$, $(2a, 2a)$, and $(2a, 0)$. The area is now $(2a)(2a) = 4a^2$, which is 4 times the area of the original square.

Similar figures

Similar figures are figures that have the same shape, but not necessarily the same size. If two figures on the coordinate plane are similar, then there is a series of transformations that can obtain one of the figures from the other. If the figures are not the same size, then one of the transformations is necessarily a dilation. If a dilation is not needed, then the two figures are not only similar, but they are also congruent. Similar figures such as polygons have corresponding side lengths that are in proportion, and corresponding angles that are congruent.

Pairs of congruent angles that are formed when two parallel lines are cut by a transversal

The diagram shows parallel lines *m* and *n* cut by transversal *T*. Angles 1 and 3 are corresponding angles. Other pairs of corresponding angles are 2 and 4, 5 and 7, and 6 and 8. Angles 2 and 6 are alternate interior angles, as are angles 3 and 7. Angles 1 and 5 are alternate exterior angles, as are angles 4 and 8. Angles 1 and 7, 2 and 8, 3 and 5, and 4 and 6 are all pairs of vertical angles. Each of these pairs of angles consists of two congruent angles.

Converse of the Pythagorean Theorem

The converse of the Pythagorean Theorem states that if the sum of the squares of the lengths of any two sides of a triangle are equal to the square of the length of the remaining side, then the triangle is a right triangle. The converse is applied when all three side lengths of a triangle are known, but the angle measures are not. The Pythagorean Theorem is applied when it is known that one angle of the triangle is a right angle, i.e., that the triangle is a right triangle. Then if two side lengths are known, the theorem can be applied to determine the missing side length.

Write two equations that could help solve for *x* and *y* in the diagram. What theorem is needed?

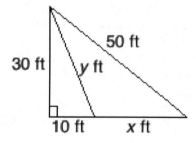

There are two right triangles in the diagram. Because *x* and *y* represent unknown lengths in the diagram, the Pythagorean Theorem can be used to solve for *x* and *y*. In the small right triangle, *y* is length of the hypotenuse. This gives the equation $30^2 + 10^2 = y^2$, or $y^2 = 1000$, so $y = 10\sqrt{10}$. In the large right triangle, the two segments labeled 10 ft and *x* ft form a leg, so the expression $(10 + x)$ represents the length of the leg. This leads to the equation $30^2 + (10 + x)^2 = 50^2$, or $(10 + x)^2 = 1600$. Since $40^2 = 1600$, $10 + x = 40$ and $x = 30$.

- 8 -

Apply the Pythagorean Theorem to find the distance from the origin to the point (*a*, *b*).

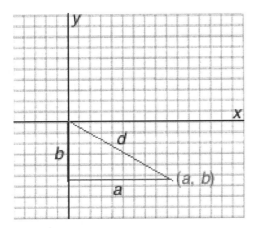

The sketch shows the point (*a*, *b*) in the fourth quadrant. Regardless of which quadrant the point is located, a right triangle can be drawn as shown. The lengths of the legs of the triangle are *a* and *b*, since the point (*a*, *b*) is *a* units from the *y*-axis and *b* units from the *x*-axis. Note that if the point (*a*, *b*) is on the *x*-axis or *y*-axis, then the distance from the origin is simply given by the value of the intercept. By the Pythagorean Theorem, $a^2 + b^2 = d^2$, and the distance is given by $d = \sqrt{a^2 + b^2}$.

Determining the weight of a bowling ball with a 4-inch radius and the material used to make the ball has a density of 0.05 lb/in³

The weight of a bowling ball can be calculated if the volume of the ball is known. The ball is in the shape of a sphere, and the formula for the volume of a sphere is $V = \frac{4}{3}\pi r^3$, where *r* is the radius of the ball. If the calculated volume is multiplied by the density of the material used, then the units of cubic inches will cancel. The resulting value is the weight of the bowling ball.

$$V = \frac{4}{3}\pi r^3 = \frac{4}{3}\pi 4^3 = \frac{256}{3}\pi$$
$$\text{weight} = \frac{256}{3}\pi \cdot 0.05 = \frac{64}{15}\pi, \text{ or about 13.4 lb}$$

Univariate and bivariate data

Univariate data consist of one data type, whereas bivariate data consist of two data types. For example, a set of data that consists of the lengths of several fish caught in a lake is univariate data. However, if that same data also include the time of day that each fish was caught, then the data are bivariate. A scatter plot shows the graph of bivariate data, with one data type on the horizontal axis and the other data type on the vertical axis. This way, the graph can be examined to see if there is any connection (or correlation) between the two data types (or in this example, between the length of the fish and the time when the fish was caught).

Sketching a best-fit line for a scatter plot with data that show a linear association

For a scatter plot with data that show a linear association, a best-fit line is a straight line that comes as close to all the data points as possible. To sketch the best-fit line, use a straightedge and draw a line through the points, trying to minimize the vertical distances of the points from the line. In general, about half of the data points should fall above the line, and half below the line. There may be points that fall directly on the line. If there are outliers in the scatter plot—points that do not seem to fit the data because they are very far from most of the data points—do not consider these points when sketching the line of best-fit.

A scatterplot shows hours studied for a test on the *x*-axis, and test scores on the *y*-axis. Interpret the slope and *y*-intercept of a best-fit line for the data.

Each point *(x, y)* represents the number of hours studied *x* and the corresponding score *y* on the test. The slope of the best-fit line is the change in *y* divided by the change in *x*, so this is the rate of change of the score per hour studied. For example, if the slope were 10, then there is an increase of 10 points per hour studied. The *y*-intercept is the score when *x* = 0, i.e., when the number of hours studied is zero. If the y-intercept were 35, for example, then the best-fit line predicts a score of 35 points for a student that does not study at all.

Distinguish frequencies from relative frequencies

A frequency is the number of times that an event occurs, or a data value falls into a certain category. When a frequency is given as a proportion or percentage of a population, this is a relative frequency. This means that relative frequencies give a better idea of how many data values fall into a certain group, *relative* to the population being studied. For example, suppose 50 students are asked to choose their favorite subject out of math, science, and history. The frequencies may be math = 14, science = 21, and history = 15. The relative frequencies would then be math = $\frac{14}{50}$ or 0.28, science = $\frac{21}{50}$ or 0.42, and history = $\frac{15}{50}$ or 0.30.

Rational number

A rational number is any number that can be expressed as a ratio of two integers $\frac{a}{b}$, where $b \neq 0$. The value of b is nonzero because division by zero is undefined. All integers are rational numbers because any integer a can be written as $\frac{a}{1}$. In addition, all decimal numbers that terminate or repeat a pattern are rational numbers, because they can be written as a ratio of two integers. The numbers –4.2, $3\frac{1}{5}$, 218, and 0 are all rational numbers. Non-examples of a rational number include π and $\sqrt{2}$, both of which cannot be written as a ratio of two integers. These numbers are called irrational numbers.

Using truncation to find a rational number written as a fraction that is within 0.001 of $\sqrt{5} = 2.360679774$ .....

Truncation refers to the removal of significant digits from the right-most decimal place of a number, typically to get an approximation.

Truncating the given value of $\sqrt{5}$ after 3 decimal places gives us 2.360. This number is accurate within 0.001 because no matter what the 4th decimal place is, it represents a value that is less than 0.001. Written as a fraction, $2.360 = 2\frac{360}{1000} = 2\frac{9}{25}$.

Why the expressions $\left(\frac{1}{2}\right)^{-2}$ and 2^2 are equivalent

To show that the expressions are equivalent, simplify each expression by using the properties of exponents. Negative exponents such as –2 can be rewritten as (2)(–1), and the exponent –1 corresponds to taking the reciprocal of the expression.

$$\left(\frac{1}{2}\right)^{-2} = \left[\left(\frac{1}{2}\right)^2\right]^{-1}$$

Use the property $a^{mn} = (a^m)^n$ to rewrite the expression.

$= \left[\frac{1}{4}\right]^{-1}$ Simplify the power.

$= 4$ The reciprocal of $\frac{1}{4}$ is 4.

The expression $2^2 = 4$, so both expressions simplify to 4 and therefore the expressions are equivalent.

Using radical notation to write the solutions to $x^3 = 16$ and $x^3 = 27$

Each equation has x raised to the power of 3. To undo this, take the cube root of each side of the equation:

$$x^3 = 16 \qquad x^3 = 27$$

$$x = \sqrt[3]{16} \qquad x = \sqrt[3]{27}$$

The numbers 16 and 27 go beneath the radical symbol. These numbers are referred to as radicands. The small 3 outside the radical symbol represents cube root. This number is called the index. The solution to the equation $x^3 = 27$ is an integer, but the solution to $x^3 = 16$ is not. $\sqrt[3]{27} = 3$ because $3^3 = 3 \cdot 3 \cdot 3 = 27$. $\sqrt[3]{16}$ is not an integer. Its value is between the integers 2 and 3, because $2^3 = 8$ and $3^3 = 27$. Using a calculator, $\sqrt[3]{16}$ is approximately 2.52.

The U.S. gross debt increased from about 5.1×10^8 dollars in 1940 to about 1.4×10^9 dollars in 2010. Estimate how many times larger the debt in 2010 is compared to the debt in 1940.

To estimate how many times larger the debt is in 2010, write the ratio of debt in 2010 to the debt in 1940. Break up the powers of 10 and use the properties of integer exponents to simplify $\frac{10^9}{10^8}$ to 10. Multiply to get $\frac{14}{5.1}$, which is equivalent to $\frac{140}{51}$. Since 51 is very close to 50, $\frac{140}{51}$ is about $\frac{140}{50} = \frac{14}{5}$ or 2.8.

$$\frac{1.4 \times 10^9}{5.1 \times 10^8} = \frac{1.4}{5.1} \cdot \frac{10^9}{10^8} = \frac{1.4}{5.1} \cdot 10 = \frac{14}{5.1} \approx \frac{14}{5} = 2.8$$

Check the estimate with a calculator: $\frac{1.4 \times 10^9}{5.1 \times 10^8} \approx 2.745098 \ldots$

Adding large numbers written in scientific notation

When adding very large numbers in scientific notation, special attention must be paid to the powers of 10. If the exponents on the powers of 10 are the same, then the numbers being multiplied by the powers of 10 can be added. The sum is then multiplied by the same power of 10, and then the product is rewritten (if necessary) in scientific notation.

If the exponents on the powers of 10 are different, then the smaller numbers should be rewritten to match the greatest power of 10. This is shown in the example below:
$3.854 \times 10^{29} + 8.066 \times 10^{28} =$
$3.854 \times 10^{29} + 0.8066 \times 10^{29}$ = Rewrite with the power 10^{29}.
4.6606×10^{29} Add the numbers and keep the power 10^{29}.

Henry drives 310 miles in 5 hours and 10 minutes. He says his distance-time graph shows a proportional relationship. What does this say about Henry's driving rate?

The proportional relationship is of the form $d = rt$, where r is a non-zero constant. This means the graph is a straight line through the origin with a slope of r. Henry is therefore driving at a constant rate equal to the slope r of the line graph. To determine the rate in miles per hour, convert 5 hours and 10 minutes to hours. There are 60 minutes in 1 hour, so 10 minutes is $\frac{1}{6}$ hour. The rate is given by the following ratio:

$$\frac{310}{5\frac{1}{6}} = 310 \cdot \frac{6}{31} = 60$$

Henry is driving at a constant rate of 60 miles per hour.

Use similar triangles to confirm that the slope of a non-vertical straight line is the same for any two distinct points on the line

Draw a non-vertical line m on the coordinate plane. Then draw 3 distinct horizontal lines intersecting line m in 3 distinct points. Finally, draw 2 vertical lines through the two intersection points just found with the greatest y-values. The graph below illustrates this.

Triangles ABC and CDE are similar by the angle-angle criterion. Angles B and D are right angles, and angle ACB and angle CED corresponding angles of two parallel line cut by transversal m. Since the triangles are similar, the ratio of CD to DE is equal to the ratio of AB to BC. These ratios are the slope of line m, which means any two points will give the same slope.

When solving a linear equation in one variable, there is no solution

When solving a linear equation in one variable, if the process results in a false equation of the form $a = b$ where a and b are different (not equal) numbers, the equation has no solution. This is because the equation is always false, independent of the value of the variable. For example, consider the solution of the equation below:

$$2x - 3(x + 1) = 2 - (x + 4)$$
$$2x - 3x - 3 = 2 - x - 4$$
$$-x - 3 = -x - 2$$
$$-3 = -2$$

For any value of x, each side of the equation evaluates to two different values. The equation therefore has no solution.

Distributive property

The distributive property is used to multiply expressions, with at least one being a parenthetical expression that has sums or differences. Algebraically, the distributive property is written as follows:

$$a(b + c) = ab + ac$$
$$(b + c)a = ba + ca$$

The distributive property is often used when solving a linear one-variable equation. This is because rewriting the products without the parentheses make it is easier to combine like terms. This is illustrated in the example below:

$$2(x - 3) = 3x - 2(x + 1)$$
$2x - 6 = 3x - 2x - 2$ Apply distributive property in two places.
$$2x - 6 = x - 2$$
$$x = 4$$

Ron graphs a system of two equations, but the graphs are the same line.

If Ron did not make a mistake, then the equations are equivalent. He should algebraically check that he can simplify one of the equations to get the other equation. If he cannot, then he may have made a mistake graphing one of the equations. If the equations are indeed equivalent, then the graph of the system is simply the graph of the line. This also means that the solution of the system is all the points on the line, and there are infinitely many solutions. Note that this is different than the solution "all real numbers"—the solution must include the equation of the line. If the line were, for example, $y = 2x + 1$, then the solution can be written $\{(x, y) \mid y = 2x + 1\}$.

Solve the system $y = x - 1$ and $y = 1 - x$ by inspection

The system $y = x - 1$ and $y = 1 - x$ can be solved by inspection, which means it can be solved by briefly studying the system and performing some mental math. The expressions $x - 1$ and $1 - x$ are opposites. In general, $a - b$ is the opposite of $b - a$, since $-(a - b) = -a + b = b - a$. This means that y is equal to some number and its opposite. The only number that is equal to its own opposite is zero, so this means $y = 0$. Substituting $y = 0$ into either equation gives $x = 1$. The solution of the system is $(x, y) = (1, 0)$.

How a system can be used to determine how 50 coins can have a value of $8, if all the coins are quarters and dimes

Let q = the number of quarters, and d = the number of dimes. This means that $q + d = 50$, because there are 50 coins altogether. To write another equation so that there is a two-variable system that can be solved, use the value of each coin. Each dime will contribute 10 cents to the $5, and each quarter will contribute 25 cents. Since $5 is equal to 500 cents, this leads to the equation $10d + 25q = 500$. Solving this system gives $d = 30$ and $q = 20$. Note that both variables must be non-negative integers; otherwise there is no solution in the context of the problem.

The graph of a relation includes the points (3, 4) and (8, 4). Determine if the relation could be a function.

Yes, the relation could be a function. In order for a relation to be a function, each input value must be assigned exactly one output value. The given points show that the input 3 is assigned 4, and the input 8 is assigned 4. It does not matter that both input values are assigned the same output value. To know for sure if the relation is a function, it must be known that every input value is assigned exactly one output value. Therefore, the relation may or may not be a function.

How can the x-intercept be determined for a linear function using a table of values for the function?

The x-intercept is the point for which $y = 0$. The x-intercept can be determined for a linear function using a table of values by first checking if the point for which $y = 0$ is in the table. If the table includes the value of x for $y = 0$, then this is the x-intercept. If this value is not in the table, try to determine the value from a pattern in the table. For example, if the y-values for $x = 1$ and $x = 2$ are known, then the difference in these values will also be the difference from $x = 0$ to $x = 1$. If no pattern can be found, calculate the change in the dependent variable divided by the change in the independent variable for two data points. The points can be any two points from the table. Then use the slope and any point from the table to determine the equation for the linear function. Once this is attained, substitute $y = 0$ into the equation and solve for x. The value of x is the x-intercept of the function.

Rearrange the equation $Ax + By = C$ to find the slope m of the line.

To find the slope of the line, write the equation in slope-intercept form, which is $y = mx + b$. When in this form, the coefficient of x is the slope of the line.

$$Ax + By = C$$
$$By = -Ax + C$$
$$y = \frac{-Ax}{B} + \frac{C}{B}$$

The coefficient of x is $-\frac{A}{B}$. This is the slope of the line, as long as $B \neq 0$. If $B = 0$, then the equation is of the form $x = \frac{C}{A}$. This is a vertical line, and therefore has undefined slope.

Finding the rate of change

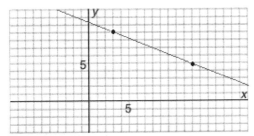

The rate of change can be determined by using any two points from the graph. Two points are given with coordinates (3, 9) and (13, 5). Calculate the slope, or rate of change, by dividing the change in y by the change in x:

$$\frac{9-5}{3-13} = \frac{4}{-10} = -\frac{2}{5}$$

The rate of change is also evident by noting the vertical distance between the points is 4 units, and the horizontal distance is 10 units. However, care must be taken to note the slope is negative, so that the correct rate of change of $-\frac{4}{10} = -\frac{2}{5}$ is determined.

Sketching a graph of a linear function that is neither decreasing nor increasing

A linear function with a positive slope is increasing, and a linear function with a negative slope is decreasing. A linear function that is neither of these must have a slope of 0. This means that the graph of the linear function is a horizontal line. A vertical line has an undefined slope, and also does not represent a function, so the graph cannot be a vertical line. An example of a graph of a horizontal line is shown below. The equation of the line is $y = -2$.

Luis says that a linear function that is rotated in the coordinate plane always results in another linear function. Determine why this is not true.

A linear function represents a line. When a line is rotated it could become vertical. A vertical line is not a function; therefore, a linear function that is rotated in the coordinate plane does not always result in another linear function.

Methods to manually test whether a reflection of an angle in the coordinate plane results in a congruent angle

To manually test if a reflection in the coordinate plane of an angle results in a congruent angle, the angle measures must be compared in some way. The first step would be two draw some triangles in the coordinate plane, and then draw some reflections over different lines. Congruent angles have equal measures. One way to then compare the angle measures would be to measure the angle measures with a protractor. If corresponding angles have the same measure, this would support the claim that angles are taken to angles with the same measure. A second way to compare the angles would be to trace the original triangles on tracing paper. Then flip the paper over, and see if the triangles can be overlaid on top of the reflected triangles.

Line *m* is parallel to line *n*. The lines are translated several units up and several units to the right, forming lines *m´* and *n´*. Name all the pairs of lines that are parallel.

Line *m* and line *n* are parallel. In addition, lines *m´* and *n´* are parallel, because translations take parallel lines to parallel lines. To know whether or not any other combinations of lines are parallel, the number of units of the translation must be known. This is because line *m* may have been taken to itself, or possibly to line *n*. Similarly, line *n* may have been taken to itself, or to line *m*. A line cannot be parallel to itself. As an example, suppose the lines have slope $\frac{2}{3}$. If the translation is up 2 units and right 3 units, each line will be taken to itself.

Segment *AB* has endpoints *A*(–1, 1) and *B*(-1, 4). Use a sequence of transformations to prove segment *AB* is congruent to segment *CD* with endpoints *C*(1, –1) and *D*(4, –1).

The segments are congruent if there is a sequence of rotations, reflections, or translations that take segment *AB* to segment *CD*. Because *AB* is a vertical segment and CD is a horizontal segment, first rotate segment *AB* clockwise 90° about the origin. The gives segment *A´B´* with endpoints *A´*(1, 1) and *B´*(4, 1). Next, translate segment *A´B´* down 2 units. This gives the segment *A´´B´´* with endpoints *A´´*(1, –1) and *B´´*(4, –1). These are the endpoints of segment *CD*, so segment *AB* is therefore congruent to segment *CD*.

Effect on the coordinates of segment *XY* after a reflection over the *y*-axis

After a reflection over the *y*-axis, the *x*-coordinates of the points of segment *XY* are multiplied by –1. This is because each point on *XY* and the corresponding point of the reflection image *X´Y´* are the same distance from the *y*-axis. For example, if point *X* has coordinates X(3, –6), then the image *X´* would have coordinates *X´*(–3, –6). Even if *XY* is on the y-axis, this will work, because the *x*-coordinates of *XY* are equal to 0. This means the x-coordinates will remain 0 when multiplied by –1, and the reflection image *X´Y´* is the same as the original pre-image *XY*.

Yolanda claims that if two figures are similar, then one can be obtained from the first by a sequence of rotations, reflections, and translations. What is wrong with her statement?

Yolanda may be thinking about congruent figures. If two figures are congruent, one can be obtained from the first by a sequence of rotations, reflections, and translations. These congruent figures are also similar. However, if two figures are similar but are not congruent, then the sequence of transformations must also include

a dilation. This is because the figures do not have the same size, despite having the same shape. If Yolanda includes dilations in her list of transformations, her statement would be correct: if two figures are similar, then one can be obtained from the first by a sequence of rotations, reflections, translations, and dilations.

Angle-angle criterion for similar triangle and does it apply to congruent triangles

The angle-angle criterion for similar triangles states that two triangles are similar if they have two congruent angles. Angles are congruent if they have the same measure. Triangles have 3 interior angles, and the sum of the measures of the angles is 180°. It follows that if two angle measures are the same in two triangles, then the 3rd angles must also be the same measure. The angle-angle criterion does not apply to congruent triangles. That is, if two triangles have two congruent angles, the triangles are not necessarily congruent, despite the fact that all 3 angles are actually congruent. For example, two equilateral triangles could have sides of 10 units and 20 units. They are not congruent triangles, but they are similar.

Melissa is reading a proof of the Pythagorean Theorem. It begins with the diagram shown. Determine how the figure will use areas to prove the theorem.

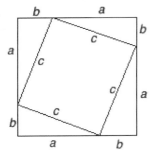

The figure shows a square with side length $a + b$. The square has an inscribed square with side length c, which also is the hypotenuse of 4 congruent right triangles. The figure can be used to write two equivalent expressions for the area of the large square, and then to write an equation to arrive at the Pythagorean Theorem.

Area of large square = $(a + b)^2$
Area of large square = area of small square and
4 triangles = $c^2 + 4 \cdot \frac{1}{2}ab$
$(a + b)^2 = c^2 + 4 \cdot \frac{1}{2}ab$
$a^2 + 2ab + b^2 = c^2 + 2ab$
$a^2 + b^2 = c^2$

A cube has a side length of 10 inches. What is the distance from one corner of the cube to the opposite corner?

10 inches

Each face of the cube is a 10-inch square. In order to determine the length of the segment from one corner to the opposite corner, first calculate the diagonal of a face of the cube using the Pythagorean Theorem.

$$10^2 + 10^2 = d^2$$
$$200 = d^2$$
$$d = \sqrt{200} = 10\sqrt{2}$$

The diagonal of the face of the cube, along with an edge of the cube, forms a right triangle with the desired segment as a hypotenuse. This gives the figure shown. Apply the Pythagorean Theorem again to find the length.

10 inches

$10\sqrt{2}$ inches

$$10^2 + \left(10\sqrt{2}\right)^2 = c^2$$
$$300 = d^2$$
$$d = \sqrt{300} = 10\sqrt{3}$$

The length from one corner to the opposite corner is $10\sqrt{3}$ inches.

Find an expression that gives the distance from (a, a) to (b, b), where $a < b$.

The distance between points (a, a) and (b, b), where $a < b$ is the length of a segment of the line $y = x$. The diagram shows two such points. Since $a < b$, the horizontal distance between the points is $b - a$. Similarly, the vertical distance between the points is $b - a$. The Pythagorean Theorem can be used to find the hypotenuse of the triangle, which is the distance from (a, a) to (b, b).

$(b - a)^2 + (b - a)^2 = d^2$
$2(b - a)^2 = d^2$

$$d = \sqrt{2(b - a)^2}$$
$$d = \sqrt{2}(b - a)$$

The distance is $\sqrt{2}(b - a)$ units.

Finding the volume of a can of soup with a radius of 1.5 inches and a height of 6 inches

A can is in the shape of a cylinder. To find the volume of the can with a radius of 1.5 inches and a height of 6 inches, use the formula for the volume of a cylinder, $V = \pi r^2 h$. The variable r represents the radius, which is 1.5 inches, and the variable h represents the height, which is 6 inches. The units for volume will be in cubic inches, since the radius and the height are given in inches.

$$V = \pi r^2 h$$
$$V = \pi(1.5)^2 \cdot 6 = 13.5\pi \approx 42.4$$

The volume of the can of soup is about 42.4 cubic inches.

Clustering in the context of a scatter plot

A scatter plot is a graph that shows data points for bivariate data. The points can be examined to see if there is any relationship between the two variables. Clustering refers to the grouping of several of the data points around a particular value or values of the data set, so much so that the data points appear to form a "cluster" on the graph. This clustering may be an indicator of an additional relationship in the data, such as a preference or most likely event. For example, a scatter plot of "age" and "ice cream cones bought" might show clustering around 25–30 years old and 3–4 ice creams, because an area has many young families with children.

Why a best-fit line may not be reasonable for data points far beyond the data in the graph

There are various reasons why a best-fit line may not be reasonable for data points far beyond the data in the graph. One reason may be limiting factors on one of the variables. For example, a scatter plot of times for a 100-meter race may show a negative linear relationship, but it is unreasonable to assume the times would continue to get faster indefinitely. Another reason may be the changes in other variables that affect the relationship in the data. For example, the cost of a 3-bedroom home may show a positive linear relationship over several years, but then decline for economic reasons.

A scatter plot shows the average temperature (°F) t in August on the horizontal axis, and the number of tornadoes n in August on the vertical axis. The best-fit line for the data is $n = 0.075t - 4$. What do the slope and n-intercept suggest about the data?

The slope of the line represents the rate of change in the number of tornadoes per 1 °F temperature change. The slope is 0.075 or $\frac{3}{40}$, which means that for each 40 °F increase in temperature, there is an additional 3 tornadoes. The n-intercept is –4, which represents –4 tornadoes for a temperature of 0 °F. These values suggest that the temperature data was probably between 70 °F and 100 °F, because a temperature of almost 70 °F is needed for the best-fit line to get a value of 1 tornado. Similarly, a temperature of over 100 °F would be needed to produce 4 tornadoes.

The table shows the results for a vote on whether the school mascot should be changed. Describe how to make a relative frequency table for the rows.

	Yes	No
Girls	36	24
Boys	48	12

To make a relative frequency table, calculate the relative frequencies for each group. Adding the frequencies shows that there are 24 + 36 = 60 girls and 48 + 12 = 60 boys that voted. The relative frequencies for the rows, or the girls and the boys, are calculated as follows:

Voted yes and is a girl: $\frac{36}{60} = 0.6$ Voted no and is a girl: $\frac{24}{60} = 0.4$

Voted yes and is a boy: $\frac{48}{60} = 0.8$ Voted no and is a boy: $\frac{12}{60} = 0.2$

	Yes	No	Total
Girls	0.6	0.4	1
Boys	0.8	0.2	1

The relative frequency table is shown, with the sums of the rows having a sum of 1.

Rational numbers

All decimal numbers that repeat a pattern or terminate (which can also be thought of as repeating zeros) are rational numbers. The definition of a rational number is any number that can be written as a ratio of two integers. To show 3.125 can be written in this form, covert the decimal 0.125 to a fraction. Since there are 3 digits after the decimal, begin by writing 0.125 as 125 over 1000:

$$0.125 = \frac{125}{1000} = \frac{5}{40} = \frac{1}{8}$$

The number 3.125 is therefore equal to the mixed fraction $3\frac{1}{8}$. Convert this fraction to an improper fraction:

$$3\frac{1}{8} = \frac{25}{8}$$

The rational number 3.125 is written as a ratio of two integers as $\frac{25}{8}$.

If n is a positive integer and n < 100, when is $\sqrt[3]{n}$ rational? The expression $\sqrt[3]{n}$ represents the cube root of the number n. This means that if $a = \sqrt[3]{n}$, then $a^3 = n$. For the expression $\sqrt[3]{n}$ to be a rational number, n must be a perfect cube. A perfect cube is the cube of an integer, such as 27: 27 = 3^3. To find the perfect cubes that are less than 100, it is easiest to cube the integers 1, 2, 3,… until the cube is greater than 99.
$1^3 = 1, 2^3 = 8, 3^3 = 27, 4^3 = 64, 5^3 = 125$

The expression $\sqrt[3]{n}$ is rational for $n < 100$ when n is 1, 8, 27, or 64.

Using the approximation $\sqrt{2} \approx 1.41$ to compare the numbers $3\sqrt{2}$ and $\frac{21}{5}$

The irrational number $3\sqrt{2}$ is equal to 3 times the number $\sqrt{2}$. Use the given approximation for $\sqrt{2}$ to write a decimal approximation for $3\sqrt{2}$:

$$3\sqrt{2} = 3 \cdot \sqrt{2} \approx 3 \cdot 1.41 = 4.23$$

The number 4.23 is a rational number approximation for the irrational number $3\sqrt{2}$. To compare this to the fraction $\frac{21}{5}$, either convert the fraction to a decimal or convert the decimal approximation to a fraction. It is easy to convert the fraction to a decimal: $\frac{21}{5} = 4\frac{1}{5} = 4.2$, or 4.20. This is slightly less than the number 4.23, so $\frac{21}{5} < 3\sqrt{2}$.

Effect of zero as an exponent using a property of integer exponents

For any non-zero number a, the expression $a^0 = 1$. If the base $a = 0$, then the expression is undefined. This meaning of zero as an exponent makes sense for all of the properties of integer exponents. For example, when multiplying two exponential expressions with the same base, the exponents are added: $a^m a^n = a^{m+n}$. If $m = 0$, then the expression would look like this:

$$a^0 a^n = a^{0+n} = a^n$$

This equation says $a^0 a^n = a^n$, which must mean that $a^0 = 1$. Similar justifications are possible for the other properties of integer exponents.

Expressing the number 5,000,000,000,000,000 as a single digit times an integer power of 10

To write the number 5,000,000,000,000,000 as a single digit times an integer power of 10, first examine some integer powers of 10:

$10^{-3} = 0.001$ $10^2 = 100$
$10^{-2} = 0.01$ $10^3 = 1{,}000$
$10^{-1} = 0.1$ $10^4 = 10{,}000$
$10^0 = 0$ $10^5 = 100{,}000$
$10^1 = 1$ $10^6 = 1{,}000{,}000$

The pattern shows that for positive integer powers of 10, when the exponent is n then the number is written as 1 followed by n zeros. The number $5{,}000{,}000{,}000{,}000{,}000 = 5 \times 1{,}000{,}000{,}000{,}000{,}000$, which has a 1 followed by 15 zeros as a factor. It follows that the number 5,000,000,000,000,000 can be written as 5×10^{15}, which is a digit times an integer power of 10.

Dividing small numbers written in scientific notation

When dividing very small numbers in scientific notation, divide the coefficients (the numbers multiplied by a power of 10) and the powers of 10 separately. That is, $\frac{a \times 10^m}{b \times 10^n} = \frac{a}{b} \cdot 10^m 10^n$. In this way, the exponent property $\frac{a^m}{a^n} = a^{m-n}$ can be applied to the powers of 10, leaving only one power of 10. If the quotient $\frac{a}{b}$ is not between 1 and 10, then adjust the expression so that the result is also in scientific notation:

$$\frac{7.80 \times 10^{-23}}{9.75 \times 10^{-19}} = \frac{7.80}{9.75} \cdot \frac{10^{-23}}{10^{-19}} = 0.8 \times 10^{-4} = 8.0 \times 10^{-5}$$

Note that $0.8 = 8.0 \times 10^{-1}$, which explains why $0.8 \times 10^{-4} = 8.0 \times 10^{-5}$.

A DVD service charges a $50 sign-up fee and $10/month for unlimited DVDs. Is the graph of total cost as a function of number of months a graph of a proportional relationship?

It is not a proportional relationship because of the sign-up fee. If y is proportional to x, then $y = kx$, where k is a non-zero constant. The DVD service charge; however, starts out with a $50 service charge (at zero months) and then increases $10 per month. The equation of this line is $y = 10x + 50$. 50 is added to the right side of the equation regardless of the value of x; therefore, the right side of the equation is not proportional to the left. Note that the line representing a proportional relationship passes through the origin where x and y both equal zero. If the DVD service did not charge a sign-up fee, it would be a proportional relationship.

Derive the equation $y = mx$ for a non-vertical line through the origin, where the slope m is the change in y divided by the change in x for any two points on the graph.

Graph a straight line through the origin (0, 0). Any point (x, y) on the line will be x units from the y-axis and y units from the x-axis, as is illustrated in the diagram. This will even be true for a horizontal line—each point will be x units from the y-axis and 0 units from the x-axis (the line *is* the x-axis).

The slope is the ratio of the change in y and the change in x, so write an equation for the slope: $m = \frac{y}{x}$, for any point (x, y) on the graph. Solving this equation for y gives $y = mx$.

Finding the value(s) of b such that $2x + 4 = b(x + 1)$

To find the value(s) of b, first solve the equation for x:

$$2x + 4 = b(x + 1)$$
$$2x + 4 = bx + b$$
$$2x - bx = b - 4$$
$$x(2 - b) = b - 4$$
$$x = \frac{b - 4}{2 - b}$$

The expression for x is undefined for $b = 2$.

It follows that the equation $2x + 4 = b(x + 1)$ has one solution and $b \neq 2$.

How a least common denominator can help to solve linear equations with fractions and fractional coefficients

When solving a linear equation with fractions and fractional coefficients, a least common denominator or LCD can simplify the operations. By multiplying each side of the equation by the LCD, the denominators of the fractions are cleared out. This results in a linear equation that has integers and integer coefficients, and it is easier to solve for the variable. This is illustrated in the following example:

$$\frac{2}{3}x + \frac{1}{5} = -x + \frac{5}{6}$$
$$30\left(\frac{2}{3}x + \frac{1}{5}\right) = 30\left(-x + \frac{5}{6}\right)$$
$$20x + 6 = -30x + 25$$
$$50x = 19$$
$$x = \frac{19}{50}$$

Ryan says the solution to the system $x + y = 4$ and $2x - y = -7$ is (3, 1). Determine if this is correct or incorrect.

A solution to a system of two linear equations is a point (x, y) that satisfies both equations of the system. In this case, Ryan found an incorrect solution because the point (3, 1) only satisfies the equation $x + y = 4$. When x = 3 and y = 1 are substituted into the equation $2x - y = -7$, the result is 5 = -7, which is false. The correct solution to the system is the point (-1, 5):

$x + y = 4$	$2x - y = -7$
$-1 + 5 = 4$	$2(-1) - (5) = -7$
$4 = 4$	$-7 = -7$

Note that there are an infinite number of solutions for either of the two equations, but only one solution for the system. This solution point corresponds to the intersection point of the graphs of the equations.

Using mental math to solve the system $2x = 1$ and $y + x = 1$

To solve a system of two linear equations using mental math or by inspection, first try to determine if either of the two equations can be solved right away. In this case, the first equation only has one variable, x. It is also a one-step equation, and is easily solved by dividing each side of the equation by 2. This results in $x = \frac{1}{2}$. The second equation states that the sum of x and y is equal to 1. It must be that $y = \frac{1}{2}$, because $\frac{1}{2} + \frac{1}{2} = 1$. This means the solution of the linear system is $\left(\frac{1}{2}, \frac{1}{2}\right)$.

Write a system that could be used to determine if and where the line through the origin and (3, 2) intersects the line through (1, 5) and (–3, 6).

Find equations for each line. The slope of the first line is $m = \frac{2-0}{3-0} = \frac{2}{3}$. Use the point-slope form of a line to find the equation:

$$y - y_0 = m(x - x_0)$$
$$y - 0 = \frac{2}{3}(x - 0)$$
$$y = \frac{2}{3}x$$

The slope of the second line is $m = \frac{6-5}{-3-1} = -\frac{1}{4}$. Use the point-slope form of a line to find the equation:

$$y - y_0 = m(x - x_0)$$
$$y - 5 = -\frac{1}{4}(x - 1)$$
$$y = -\frac{1}{4}x + \frac{21}{4}$$

Since the slopes of the two lines are different, they do intersect. The system $y = \frac{2}{3}x$ and $y = -\frac{1}{4}x + \frac{21}{4}$ can be used to determine the point of intersection.

A computer takes an input from the set {1, 2, 3}. The output is a number from {0, 1, 2, 3} that is less than the input number. Is this set of all possible pairs of inputs and outputs a function?

A function is a relation such that each input value is assigned exactly one output value. If the computer takes the input 1, only one number in the output set is less than 1, the number 0. However, for any other input, there are multiple possible output values. For example, if the input is 2, then the numbers 0 and 1 are possible outputs. This means that (2, 0) and (2, 1) are in the set of all possible pairs of inputs and outputs. For this reason, the set of all possible pairs of inputs and outputs is not a function.

Company A increases sales by 30% each year since 2010. Company B has yearly sales described by the function s = 14,000 + 6,000t, where t is the number of years since 2010. Compare the sales growth of the companies.

We don't know how much Company A's sales are, but we know that they increase by an amount equal to 30% of the prior year's sales for each year after 2010. Company B on the other hand has $14,000 in sales in 2010, and an additional $6,000 in sales for each succeeding year. So its sales growth percentage, rounded to the nearest percent, is as follows:

$$\text{2011 Sales Growth \%} = \frac{\text{2011 Sales Growth}}{\text{2010 Sales}} = \frac{6,000}{14,000} = 43\%$$
$$\text{2012 Sales Growth \%} = \frac{\text{2012 Sales Growth}}{\text{2011 Sales}} = \frac{6,000}{20,000} = 30\%$$
$$\text{2013 Sales Growth \%} = \frac{\text{2013 Sales Growth}}{\text{2012 Sales}} = \frac{6,000}{26,000} = 24\%$$

- 24 -

$$\text{2014 Sales Growth \%} = \frac{\text{2014 Sales Growth}}{\text{2013 Sales}} = \frac{6{,}000}{32{,}000} = 19\%$$

So Company B's Growth % starts out higher than Company A's, but then becomes less.

Jill is given two points of a function. She graphs the points. Because she can draw a straight line through the two points, she decides the function is linear. Explain Jill's error.

Jill did not graph enough points to determine if the graph is linear. In fact, there is a straight line through any two distinct points on the coordinate plane. If a function represents a linear relationship, then all points of the function will fall on the same straight line. If Jill had at least graphed 3 points, she may have been able to determine if the function is *not* linear. This would be evident by all 3 points not lying on a straight line. Note, however, that no matter how many points are graphed and fall on a straight line, it is still possible that the function is not linear.

What is the rate of change of the linear function?

The data in the table represent a linear function. For a linear function, the rate of change is equal to the slope. To find the slope, calculate the change in y divided by the change in x for any two points from the table:

x	y
3	8
−1	14
−3	17

$$m = \frac{14 - 8}{-1 - 3} = \frac{6}{-4} = -\frac{3}{2}$$

Note that this value is the same for any two points from the table:

$$m = \frac{17 - 8}{-3 - 3} = \frac{9}{-6} = -\frac{3}{2}$$

The rate of change of the linear function is $-\frac{3}{2}$. Remember to subtract in the same direction for the y-values and x-values. This ensures the correct sign of the rate of change. For example, if the difference −1 − 3 above were written as 3 − (−1) = 4, the slope would have come out to be $\frac{3}{2}$.

A graph of a function is shown. Is it linear or nonlinear? When is the function increasing or decreasing?

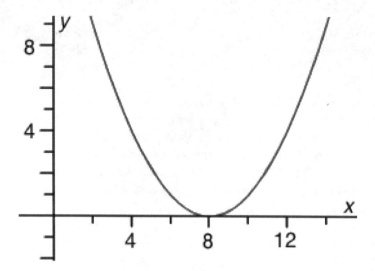

The function is nonlinear. If the function were linear, all of the points would fall in a straight line, resulting in a line graph. Any graph that is curved represents a nonlinear function. The function is increasing when the graph rises from left to right. Similarly, the function is decreasing when the graph falls from left to right. The graph appears to change from decreasing to increasing at the point $(8, 0)$. This means that for $x < 8$, the function is decreasing. For $x > 8$, the function is increasing.

A right triangle in the coordinate plane has a hypotenuse with length 20 units. The triangle is translated 5 units down. What is the length of the hypotenuse of the translated triangle?

A two-dimensional figure is congruent to another if the second can be obtained from the first by a sequence of rotations, reflections, and translations. The triangle was translated, so the resulting triangle is congruent to the original triangle. Congruent figures have corresponding parts that are congruent, so the hypotenuses of the two triangles are congruent. This means that the length of the hypotenuse of the translated triangle is also 20 units. Note that the distance and direction that the triangle is translated in has no effect on the length of the hypotenuse, or any of the sides of the triangle.

Describe the effect on the coordinates of a point of a figure if the figure is rotated 90° clockwise about the origin.

When a figure is rotated 90° clockwise about the origin, each point (x, y) is taken to the point $(y, -x)$. This is illustrated by the points $(-4, -7)$ and $(5, 2)$ in the diagram, which are taken to $(-7, 4)$ and $(2, -5)$ respectively. This could further be illustrated using points on the x-axis or y-axis. For example, the point $(5, 0)$ will be taken to the point $(0, -5)$, and the point $(10, 0)$ will be taken to the point $(0, -10)$. Points on the x-axis are taken to the y-axis, and vice-versa.

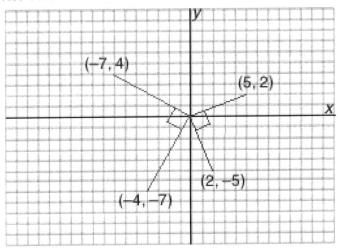

Is the rectangle with vertices $A(0, 0)$, $B(0, 4)$, $C(3, 4)$, and $D(3, 0)$ similar to the rectangle with vertices $F(0, 0)$, $G(0, 6)$, $H(4.5, 6)$, and $I(4.5, 0)$?

Yes, the two rectangles are similar figures. A two-dimensional figure is similar to another if the second can be obtained from the first by a sequence of rotations, reflections, translations, and dilations. Each coordinate of the vertices of rectangle $ABCD$ was multiplied by 1.5 to get each coordinate of the vertices of rectangle $FGHI$. This means that rectangle $FGHI$ is a dilation of rectangle $ABCD$ by a factor of 1.5. Another way to verify the figures are similar is to note that both rectangles have 4 congruent right angles, and the ratios of corresponding side lengths are equal.

A triangle has angle measures as follows: $m\angle A = a°$, $m\angle B = b°$, and $m\angle C = c°$. Write an expression for the measure of the exterior angle at angle A.

An expression for the measure of the exterior angle at angle A is $(b + c)°$. The sum of the measures of the interior angles of any triangle is 180°. This means that $a + b + c = 180$. Now let x = the measure of the exterior angle at angle A. Because the exterior angle and angle A form a linear pair, the sum of the measures of these angles is 180°. This means that $x + a = 180$. Substitution gives the equation $x + a = a + b + c$, and therefore $x = b + c$.

A triangle has side lengths of 3 cm, $\sqrt{5}$ cm, and $\sqrt{14}$ cm. Is the triangle a right triangle?

The converse of the Pythagorean Theorem states that if the sum of the squares of the lengths of any two sides of a triangle are equal to the square of the length of the remaining side, then the triangle is a right triangle. For the given lengths to satisfy this statement, the longest length, or $\sqrt{14}$ cm, must be the hypotenuse. 3 cm and $\sqrt{5}$ cm are the lengths of the legs. Check to see if the statement is true:

$$(3)^2 + \left(\sqrt{5}\right)^2 = \left(\sqrt{14}\right)^2$$
$$9 + 5 = 14$$
$$14 = 14$$

The equation is true, so the triangle is a right triangle.

An isosceles right triangle has a hypotenuse of 10 units. What is the area of the triangle?

An isosceles right triangle has congruent leg lengths. Apply the Pythagorean Theorem, which states that the sum of the squares of the lengths of the legs is equal to the square of the length of the hypotenuse:

$a^2 + b^2 = c^2$ Pythagorean Theorem
$b^2 + b^2 = 10^2$ The legs are congruent, so use b for each leg length.
$2b^2 = 100$
$b^2 = 50$
$b = \sqrt{50}$

The area of the triangle is one half the base times the height, or in this case $A = \frac{1}{2}b^2$, where $b^2 = 50$. The area of the triangle is therefore 25 square units.

Use the Pythagorean Theorem to find the length of segment *RU*.

First, identify the coordinates of points *R* and *U*. Point *R* has coordinates *R*(3, 7) and point *U* has coordinates *U*(6, 4). To apply the Pythagorean Theorem, draw a vertical segment down from point *R* and a horizontal segment left from point *U* to form a right triangle with *RU* as its hypotenuse. The lengths of the legs of the triangle are the difference between the *x*-coordinates and the difference between the *y*-coordinates of points *R* and *U*:

vertical leg length = 7 – 4 = 3 units

horizontal leg length = 6 – 3 = 3 units

By the Pythagorean Theorem, the length of segment *RU* is $\sqrt{3^2 + 3^2} = \sqrt{18}$ units.

Similarities between the formulas for the volume of a cylinder and the volume of a cone

The formula for the volume of a cylinder is $V = \pi r^2 h$, where r is the radius of the circular base and h is the height. The formula for the volume of a cone is $V = \frac{1}{3}\pi r^2 h$, where r is the radius of the circular base and h is the height. This means that a cone that has the same circular base and height as a cylinder has exactly one third the volume of the cylinder. If the cone were placed inside the cylinder, it would occupy one third of the interior space.

Outlier of a data set

An outlier of a data set is a data point that is very far from most of the data points. A data set may have more than one outlier, but there should not be many, as then the supposed outliers may actually be representative of the population. In general, when a sample of data is taken from a population, it is best to throw away outliers before making any conclusions about the data. An outlier could be the result of an error. For example, if various measures were taken with a 60-inch tape measure, and most values were around 39 inches, a value of 21 inches is likely from the measurer misreading the tape measure.

Knowing when a scatter plot suggests a linear association

The phrase "suggests a linear association" means that the data appear to show a pattern that follows a straight line. This means that a best-fit line should function as a good predictor for data points that fall between given data, or beyond the given data. It does not mean that the data points actually fall on a line, only that the points are all close to a line. The line may have a positive or negative slope, or even appear horizontal or vertical. Data that does not show a linear correlation may show no correlation, which means the points appear to be dispersed randomly on the graph. Alternatively, the data may show some other type of association, such as a quadratic or exponential association. Such data points will appear to follow a curve that is not straight.

A scatter plot shows the money spent at a mall as a function of the time spent in the mall for several customers. Interpret the meaning of a positive or negative slope for the best-fit line of the data.

Suppose the scatter plot of the money spent at a mall as a function of the time spent in the mall has a best-fit line with a positive slope. This means that the more time spent at the mall, the more a customer spends at the mall. This may mean customers are spending a lot of time comparing expensive items before finally making a purchase. If, on the other hand, the slope is negative, then the more time spent at the mall, the less a customer spends. This means that customers come to the mall with a purpose to buy something and then leave, or are hanging out and not spending much money at all. In either case, the slope represents money spent per hour, described as a rate of change.

Millie is watching students open and go through a set of double doors at the school. Her data is shown in the table.

	Left Door	Right Door
Left Hand	28	13
Right Hand	50	78

The data in the table shows that most students will open the door on the right when they approach the double doors. This is because $13 + 78 = 91$ students open the right door, whereas $28 + 50 = 78$ open the left door. A greater difference than this is seen in which hand is used to open the door. Over 3 times as many students open the door with the right hand, because $50 + 78 = 128$ and $28 + 13 = 41$. Overall, most students elect to open the right door with the right hand, because 78 is the greatest entry in the table.

Is the product of two irrational numbers always irrational ?

The product of two irrational numbers is NOT always irrational. It is easiest to prove a statement like this as false by finding a counterexample. If there is even one pair of irrational numbers that multiply to be a rational number, then this disproves the statement. Consider the irrational number $\sqrt{2}$. When the number is multiplied by itself, the result is 2: $\sqrt{2} \cdot \sqrt{2} = 2$. The number 2 is a rational number, because it can be written as $\frac{2}{1}$, which is a ratio of integers. In fact, if $\sqrt{n}$ is irrational for some positive integer n, then multiplying this number by itself always results in the rational number n.

The numbers 3.14 and $\frac{22}{7}$ can be used to approximate π. Which is more accurate?

In order to determine which number is a more accurate representation of the irrational number π, first write π to several decimal places, using a calculator:
$$\pi = 3.141592 \ldots$$
To make the comparison, next write the number $\frac{22}{7}$ as a decimal, so that all three values are written in decimal form:
$$\frac{22}{7} = 3.\overline{142857}$$
Write the decimals in order in a column, to better examine them:
3.140000
3.141592
3.142857

The approximations begin to differ from π in the 3rd decimal place, but both differences are 0.001, so it's not yet apparent which approximation is closest. If the 4th decimal place is included, the differences become 0.0015 and 0.0013. Therefore $\frac{22}{7}$ is a better approximation.

If n is a positive integer, are $(-3)^n$ and -3^n equivalent expressions?

To evaluate $(-3)^n$ and -3^n, both the properties of integer exponents and the order of operations must be used. Since expressions in parentheses are evaluated first, the expression $(-3)^n$ represents a product of n factors of -3, and the result will be either positive or negative depending on whether n is even or odd. The expression -3^n, however,

- 30 -

must have the exponent evaluated first. So, the expression -3^n is always negative. Since $(-3)^n$ is only negative for odd values of n the two expressions are equivalent only for odd values of n.

If n is a positive integer and $3n < 100$, for what values of n is $\sqrt{3n}$ rational?

$\sqrt{3n}$ is rational when $3n$ is a perfect square. The perfect squares that are less than 100 are: 1, 4, 9, 25, 36, 49, 64, and 81. Since n is an integer, the possible values for n are 3, 12, and 27. It can also be noted that in order for $3n$ to be a perfect square, n must be 3 times a perfect square. Therefore, possible values of n are:
$n = 3(1^2) = 3$
$n = 3(2^2) = 12$
$n = 3(3^2) = 27$

The expression $\sqrt{3n}$ is rational for $3n < 100$ when n is 3, 12, or 27.

An *astronomical unit* is a unit of length equal to about 149,597,871 kilometers. Estimate this length by writing it as a single digit times a power of 10.

To estimate 149,597,871 kilometers as a single digit times a power of 10, first determine the power of 10. A single digit means an integer from 1 to 9, so the decimal place must move to the left until the value of the number is between 1 and 10. For 149,597,871, move 8 places: 1.49597871. Now multiply this number times 10^8 to make up for moving the decimal 8 places to the left:
$149,597,871 = 1.49597871 \times 10^8$. Finally, to estimate with a single digit, we round 1.49597871 down to 1, because $4 < 5$. This gives
1×10^8.

Can the product $(3.5 \times 10^9)(4.0 \times 10^{12})$ be simplified using the distributive property? If not, what properties can be used?

No, the product $(3.5 \times 10^9)(4.0 \times 10^{12})$ cannot be simplified using the distributive property. The distributive property is used when one of the factors in a product involves the sum or difference of two or more terms. The given product only involves multiplication, and could be written without parentheses as follows:
$3.5 \times 10^9 \times 4.0 \times 10^{12}$

The order of the factors can then be rearranged by applying the commutative property of multiplication. Then the associative property of multiplication allows multiplying the powers of 10 and the other numbers separately:
$3.5 \times 10^9 \times 4.0 \times 10^{12} =$
$3.5 \times 4.0 \times 10^9 \times 10^{12} =$ Commutative Property
$(3.5 \times 4.0) \times (10^9 \times 10^{12}) =$ Associative Property
$14 \times 10^{21} = 1.4 \times 10^{22}$ Add exponents, write in scientific notation.

If 7 pounds of bananas cost $5.53, what is the unit rate? How does it relate to a graph that describes this relationship?

A rate is a ratio that relates one unit to another. This rate is a unit rate when the denominator is equal to 1. If 7 pounds of bananas cost $5.53, then the rate is $5.53 per 7 pounds of bananas. Dividing gives the unit rate: $5.53 \div 7 = 0.79$, so the unit rate is $.79 per pound. Note that a fraction can still describe a unit rate. For example, a rate of $\frac{3}{4}$ mile per minute is a unit rate, because the rate is per 1 minute.

The slope of the graph representing the cost of several pounds of bananas is equal to the unit rate. This is because the slope
$m = \frac{\text{change in cost}}{\text{change in bananas}}$ for any two points on the graph, which will always give 0.79.

Derive the equation $y = mx + b$ for a non-vertical line, where m is the slope and b is the y-intercept.

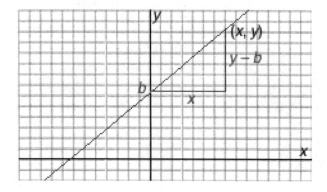

Graph a straight line through the point $(0, b)$. Draw a right triangle with a point (x, y) on the line and $(0, b)$ as the endpoints of the hypotenuse, as is illustrated in the diagram. The leg lengths of the triangle are therefore x and $y - b$.

The slope is the ratio of the change in y and the change in x, so write an equation for the slope: $m = \frac{y-b}{x}$, for any point (x, y) on the graph. Solving this equation for y gives $y = mx + b$. Note that for a horizontal line, $y - b = 0$ which simply gives the equation $y = b$.

Find the value(s) of b such that $3x - 2b = 3x + 3$ has all real numbers as its solution

To find the value(s) of b, first solve the equation for x:
$3x - 2b = 3x + 3$
$-2b = 3$

The x-terms of the equation have cancelled out. When this happens, if the resulting equation is false, there is no solution. If the resulting equation is true, then all real numbers is the solution. Since all real numbers is the desired solution, solve the equation to find the value of b that makes the equation true:
$$-2b = 3$$
$$b = -\frac{3}{2}$$

- 32 -

The equation has all real numbers as its solution when $b = -\frac{3}{2}$. Notice that the equation becomes 3x + 3 = 3x + 3, which is an identity. For any value of x, each side of the equation is equal to 3.

Rational number coefficient

A coefficient is the real number factor of a variable term. For example, in the term $-3x^3y^2$ and the term 10b, the coefficients are –3 and 10, respectively. A rational number coefficient is a coefficient that is a rational number, which is a number than can be written as a ratio of two integers. –3 and 10 are therefore examples of rational number coefficients. In the term $x\sqrt{2}$, the coefficient $\sqrt{2}$ is not a rational number, so $\sqrt{2}$ is not a rational number coefficient. When like terms with rational number coefficients are combined, it is the rational number coefficients that are added or subtracted, keeping the same variable component. For example, 3x + 7x = (3 + 7)x = 10x. The same is true when combining like terms with irrational number coefficients.

Ilene says the linear system representing by the graph has no solution. Explain Ilene's error.

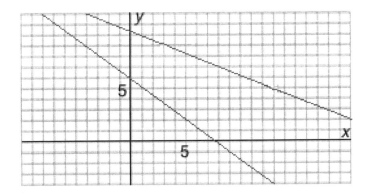

Ilene assumed that because the lines do not have a visible intersection point on the graph, the lines do not intersect. When a linear system is graphed and the lines do not intersect, or are parallel, then the system has no solution. However, it is clear from the graph that the lines will intersect, and that the lines are not parallel. The intersection point will be in the second quadrant. To find the solution of the system, either another graph is needed that shows the intersection point, or the equations for the lines can be used to find the solution algebraically. Note that even lines that appear to be parallel may not be. The slopes must be proven to be equal to know the lines are parallel.

How the system x – 2y = –4 and x + 2y = 6 can be solved by adding the equations together

The solution to a linear system of two equations must make both equations true. Two true equations when added together form a 3rd true equation. For example, 3 = 3 and 8 = 8, so it follows that
3 + 8 = 3 + 8. Write the equations vertically and add them:
x – 2y = –4
x + 2y = 6 +

$$2x \quad = 2$$
$$x = 1$$

The y-terms cancel, which gives the equation $2x = 2$, so $x = 1$. Substitute 1 for x in either of the original equations to see that $y = 2.5$. The solution is $(1, 2.5)$.

How a system of two non-parallel linear equations that is intended to represent a real-world situation might have no valid solution.

When a real-world situation is represented by a system of two linear equations, the system can be mathematically solved, but care must be taken to make sure the solution makes sense in the context of the problem. For example, a value that represents the number of people at a concert cannot be 480.5, and a value that represents the distance across a river cannot be –20. When this happens, it means that there is no valid solution to the problem, even if the system has a correct numerical solution. Of course, if a legitimate solution is expected, check to make sure the system was both written correctly and solved correctly.

Ray says that $y = x^2$ is not a function. This is because $x = 2$ gives $y = 4$ and $x = -2$ gives $y = 4$. Is Ray correct?

Ray is not correct. A function is a rule that assigns to each input exactly one output. In Ray's example, the input 2 is assigned the output 4, and the input –2 is assigned the output 4. This does not contradict the definition of a function. In order to find an example to show $y = x^2$ is not a function, Ray would have to find an x-value that gives two different y-values, which he cannot do for $y = x^2$.

A function takes an input, adds 1, then doubles the result. Another function is described by the equation $y = 2x + 2$

In order to compare these functions, determine the algebraic equation that represents the verbal description "takes an input, adds 1, then doubles the result." First, begin with the function $y = x$, where x is the input. Then add 1: $y = x + 1$. Then to double the result, which is represented by x + 1, multiply by 2: $y = 2(x + 1)$. At first, the two functions appear to be different, but using the distributive property gives $y = 2(x + 1) = 2x + 2$. The functions are actually the same function.

Does the equation $y = \frac{2x-3}{5}$ represent a linear function?

Yes, the equation $y = \frac{2x-3}{5}$ represents a linear function. The equation
$y = mx + b$ defines a linear function, and the given equation can be manipulated to be put in this form:

$$y = \frac{2x - 3}{5}$$
$$y = \frac{2x}{5} - \frac{3}{5}$$
$$y = \frac{2}{5}x - \frac{3}{5}$$

- 34 -

Written in this form, the value of m is $\frac{2}{5}$, which represents the slope of the line. The value of b is $-\frac{3}{5}$, which represents the y-intercept of the line. Any equation that can be transformed into the form $y = mx + b$ represent a linear function. Another common form is $Ax + By = C$, where A, B, and C are real numbers and $B \neq 0$.

The table shows some data points for a linear function. What is the missing value in the table?

x	y
0	
3	50
5	80

The data in the table represent a linear function. For a linear function, the rate of change is equal to the slope. To find the slope, calculate the change in y divided by the change in x for the two given points from the table:

$$m = \frac{80-50}{5-3} = \frac{30}{2} = 15$$

The rate of change of the linear function is 15. This means for each increase of 1 in the value of x, the value of y increases by 15. Similarly, each decrease of 1 in the value of x decreases the value of y by 15. The x-value 0 is 3 less than 3, so subtract $3 \cdot 15 = 45$ from 50 to get $y = 5$. This is the missing value in the table.

Sketch a graph that is nonlinear, increasing, and passes through (0, 0).

A graph that is nonlinear will not be a straight line. Also, a graph that is increasing must rise from left to right over its entire domain. For the graph to pass through the point (0, 0), draw a curve that is increasing in the third quadrant and heading toward the origin. Pass through the origin, and continue increasing into the first quadrant. A simple function that has a graph like this is the function $y = x^3$. A sketch of the graph is shown.

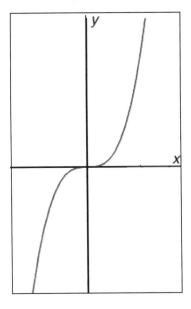

- 35 -

Give a sequence of transformations to show that figure *ABCD* is congruent to figure *MEFG*.

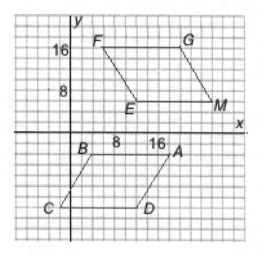

Figure *ABCD* is congruent to figure *MEFG* if there is a sequence of rotations, reflections, or translations that take figure *ABCD* to figure *MEFG*. First, translate figure *ABCD* 8 units to the right and 2 units down. Note that each square on the grid represents 2 units. Then reflect the translated figure over the x-axis, which results in figure *MEFG*. To check the transformations, apply them to the coordinates of the vertices of figure *ABCD*:

- $A(18, -4) \rightarrow (26, -6) \rightarrow (26, 6)$, which is point *M*
- $B(4, -4) \rightarrow (12, -6) \rightarrow (12, 6)$, which is point *E*
- $C(-2, -14) \rightarrow (6, -16) \rightarrow (6, 16)$, which is point *F*
- $D(12, -14) \rightarrow (20, -16) \rightarrow (20, 16)$, which is point *G*

Effect on the coordinates of triangle *GRT* after a reflection over the x-axis

After a reflection over the x-axis, the y-coordinates of the points of triangle *GRT* are multiplied by –1. This is because each point on triangle *GRT* and the corresponding point of the reflection image *G′R′T′* are the same distance from the x-axis. For example, if point *G* has coordinates $G(-2, 3)$, then the image *G′* would have coordinates $G'(-2, -3)$. Even if a vertex is on the x-axis, this will work, because the y-coordinate of the vertex is 0. This means the y-coordinate will remain 0 when multiplied by –1, and the reflection image of the vertex is the same as the original pre-image.

Any two squares are similar

A square is similar to another square if the second can be obtained from the first by a sequence of rotations, reflections, translations, and dilations. Suppose square *ABCD* in the coordinate plane has vertex $A(x, y)$, and that square *WXYZ* has vertex $W(m, n)$. Translate square *ABCD* so that vertex *A* coincides with vertex *W*. The translation will be $m - x$ units to the left or right, and $n - y$ units up or down, where the sign of the difference indicates the direction. For example, if $m - x = -3$, translate 3 units left. Then rotate square *ABCD* about the vertex *A* until point *B* is on side *WX*. Finally, dilate square *ABCD* by the factor $\frac{WX}{AB}$, with center at vertex *A*.

- 36 -

The angle measures of a triangle are in the ratio 2:3:4. What are the angle measures of the triangle?

Let the smallest angle measure of the triangle be represented by the expression $2x$. Using the ratio 2:3:4, the other two angle measures are given by the expressions $3x$ and $4x$. The sum of the interior angle measures of a triangle is 180°. Write an equation to represent this:
$2x + 3x + 4x = 180$
$9x = 180$
$x = 20$

To find the angle measures, substitute the value of x for each expression. The angle measures are $2 \cdot 20 = 40°$, $3 \cdot 20 = 60°$, and $4 \cdot 20 = 80°$.

Converse of a mathematical statement

The converse of a mathematical statement switches the hypotheses of the statement with its conclusion. For example, the Pythagorean Theorem states that if a triangle is a right triangle, then the sum of the squares of the leg lengths is equal to the square of the length of the hypotenuse. The converse states that if the sum of the squares of the leg lengths is equal to the square of the length of the hypotenuse, then the triangle is a right triangle. In this specific instance the converse is true, but in general the converse of a true statement is not necessarily true. For example, if $x = 2$, then $x^2 = 4$. The converse is if $x^2 = 4$, then $x = 2$. This is false, because $x = -2$ or $x = 2$.

A right triangle has side lengths 3 units and $\sqrt{8}$ units. What are the possible lengths of the remaining side?

There are two possibilities for the given side lengths of 3 units and $\sqrt{8}$ units. These could be the lengths of the legs of the right triangle. Or 3 could be the length of the hypotenuse of the right triangle. Note $\sqrt{8}$ cannot be the length of the hypotenuse, because $\sqrt{8} < 3$. Use the Pythagorean Theorem to find the two possible lengths:
$$a^2 + b^2 = c^2$$
$$\left(\sqrt{8}\right)^2 + 3^2 = c^2$$
$$c^2 = 8 + 9$$
$$c = \sqrt{17}$$

$$a^2 + b^2 = c^2$$
$$\left(\sqrt{8}\right)^2 + b^2 = 3^2$$
$$b^2 = 9 - 8$$
$$b = 1$$

The two possible side lengths are $\sqrt{17}$ units (the missing side length is the hypotenuse) and 1 unit (the missing side length is a leg).

The distance from $(1, a)$ to $(4, 5)$ is 5 units. Find the value of a.

The distance formula states that the distance between two points (x_1, y_1) and (x_2, y_2) is $\sqrt{(x_2 - x_1)^2 + (y_2 - y_1)^2}$. Write an equation using the given points and distance 5 units:

$$d = \sqrt{(x_2 - x_1)^2 + (y_2 - y_1)^2}$$
$$5 = \sqrt{(4 - 1)^2 + (5 - a)^2}$$
$$25 = 9 + (5 - a)^2$$
$$16 = (5 - a)^2$$
$$\pm 4 = 5 - a$$
$$a = 1 \; or \; a = 9$$

The distance from $(1, 1)$ to $(4, 5)$ is 5 units, and the distance from $(1, 9)$ to $(4, 5)$ is 5 units

A large pile of stones is approximately in the shape of a cone. How can the volume of stones be estimated?

The formula for the volume of a cone is $V = \frac{1}{3}\pi r^2 h$, where r is the radius of the circular base and h is the height. First, estimate the height of the pile by measuring it. If the pile is too tall to measure directly, estimate the leg lengths of a corner of the pile, and then set up a ratio to estimate the height of the pile:

- Measure a and b, a corner of the pile. Measure r, the radius of the pile. Estimate the height h of the pile using the ratio $\frac{a}{b} = \frac{h}{r}$.

The radius r can be measured as half the distance across the base of the pile. Alternatively, if the circumference of the base can be measured, use the equation $C = 2\pi r$ to estimate the value of r.

Tim collects data on the temperature over two weeks in the summer, and creates a scatter plot. The independent variable is the number of hours into the day (for example, 2 p.m. would be 14) and the dependent variable is the temperature in °F. Would a best-fit line likely approximate the data well?

It is unlikely that a best-fit line will approximate the data well. The reason is that for a best-fit line is used to model a relationship that shows a linear association. In general, temperatures do not steadily increase or decrease from early in the morning to late at night. There is usually a high temperature that occurs sometime in the middle of the day. For this reason, a nonlinear association is more likely to represent the data. This means there is still a relationship between the data, it is just not a linear relationship. It is possible that the scatter plot shows a linear relationship if perhaps the independent variable was only for certain times of the day, such as from 6 a.m. to noon.

The table shows the results for a survey on preferred school lunches

	Pizza	Hot Dog	Taco
Grade 6	85	105	80
Grade 7	95	90	90
Grade 8	120	70	80

To make a relative frequency table, calculate the relative frequencies for each group. Adding the frequencies shows that 85 + 95 + 120 = 300 students prefer pizza, 105 + 90 + 70 = 265 prefer hot dogs, and 80 + 90 + 80 = 250 students prefer tacos. The relative frequencies for the columns, such as pizza, are calculated as follows:

Grade 6 and prefers pizza: $\frac{85}{300} \approx 0.28$

Grade 7 and prefers pizza: $\frac{95}{300} \approx 0.32$

Grade 8 and prefers pizza: $\frac{120}{300} = 0.4$

The other relative frequencies are calculated similarly. The relative frequency table is shown, with the sums of the columns having a sum of 1.

	Pizza	Hot Dog	Taco
Grade 6	0.28	0.40	0.32
Grade 7	0.32	0.34	0.36
Grade 8	0.40	0.26	0.32
Total	1	1	1

Barry says the decimal 0.101001000100001… must be rational, because of the pattern in the digits. What is Barry's error?

A rational number is a number that can be written as a ratio of integers. The decimal representation of a rational number always eventually repeats. This means that the pattern is a finite number of digits that appear over and over again, with no other digits. For example, the decimal 3.852852852… repeats the digits 852 and therefore this number represents a rational number. Also, the decimal 5.61 is rational, because after the 1 there is a pattern of repeating zeros, which typically are not written. The decimal 0.101001000100001… does not, however, have a repeating pattern. The pattern is that the number of zeros between the 1s keeps increasing by 1, but this does not make the decimal a rational number.

Using mental math, estimate the value of the product $(2.48 \times 10^{17})(1.98 \times 10^{23})$

First, estimate the product of 2.48 and 1.98. This can be done first, because the order of the multiplication does not matter. 2.48 is about 2.5, and 1.98 is about 2, so 2.48×1.98 is about $2.5 \times 2 = 5$. Next, multiply the powers of 10. This is a simple application of the multiplication property of exponents, which states that $a^m a^n = a^{m+n}$. So $10^{17} \times 10^{23}$ is equal to 10^{40}. Therefore the product $(2.48 \times 10^{17})(1.98 \times 10^{23})$ is approximately equal to 5×10^{40}.

The solution to 4(x + A) = 2Ax + B is *all real numbers*. What are the value of A and B?

To find the values of A and B, first expand the linear equation x:
$$4(x + A) = 2Ax + B$$
$$4x + 4A = 2Ax + B$$

When a linear equation has the solution all real numbers, it means that the equation is an identity. In other words, both sides of the equation are the same algebraic expression. The left side of the equation has the term $4x$, and therefore the right hand side must also have this expression:
$$4x = 2Ax$$
$$4 = 2A$$
$$A = 2$$

The value of A is 2. This means the left side of the equation is the expression $4x + 8$. Since the constant term is 8, the constant on the right hand side of the equation must be 8. Therefore, $B = 8$. The identity is $4x + 8 = 4x + 8$.

Today, Tom is 8 years older than Janet. In 3 years, Tom will be twice as old as Janet. How old is Janet today?

The situation can be represented with a system of linear equations. Let t = Tom's age today and j = Janet's age today. Their ages in 3 years will therefore be $t + 3$ and $j + 3$. Write equations relating their ages today, and their ages in 3 years.
$t = j + 8$ Tom is 8 years older than Janet today.
$t + 3 = 2(j + 3)$ In 3 years, Tom's age ($t + 3$) is two times Janet's age ($j + 3$).
Substitute the expression j + 8 for t in the second equation:
$$t + 3 = 2(j + 3)$$
$$(j + 8) + 3 = 2(j + 3)$$
$$j + 11 = 2j + 6$$
$$j = 5$$

Today, Janet is 5 years old.

Vertical line test for testing whether a relation is a function

The vertical line test can be used to test whether a relation is a function, when a graph of the relation is given. For each input of a function, there is exactly one output. Since the inputs are represented on the horizontal axis, any vertical line must pass through the function at most one time. If the vertical line passes through the function twice, then that particular input (on the horizontal axis) would have two distinct corresponding outputs. This would mean the relation does not represent a function. Note that the vertical line test can be used to quickly rule out a relation as a function, but a graph that passes the vertical line test is not necessarily proven to be a function. It would depend on whether the behavior of the entire graph was known for all input values.

Determine how the slope of a linear graph relates to whether the graph is increasing, decreasing, or neither.

The slope of a linear graph represents the rate of change of the dependent variable per the change in the independent variable. The horizontal axis, on which we measure the independent value (the x value) increases to the right. The vertical axis, on which we measure the dependent value (the y value) increases upwards. Therefore, a graph that increases (goes up) from left to right has a positive slope, and a graph that decreases (goes down) from left to right has a negative slope. If a linear graph is neither increasing nor decreasing, then the rate of change is zero. This means that the slope of the graph is zero, and the graph is a horizontal line.

A segment with endpoints A(0, 10) and B(6, 0) is dilated by a factor of 0.5 with the origin as the center of dilation. Compare the lengths of AB and A´B´.

In order to compare the lengths of AB and A´B´, first find the coordinates of points A´ and B´. A dilation of 0.5 with the origin as the center of dilation will multiply the coordinates of A(0, 10) and B(6, 0) by 0.5. This gives A´(0, 5) and B´(3, 0). Sketch the segments in the coordinate plane:

Using the Pythagorean Theorem, the length of each segment can be determined:
$$AB = \sqrt{6^2 + 10^2} = \sqrt{136} = 2\sqrt{34}$$
$$A'B' = \sqrt{3^2 + 5^2} = \sqrt{34}$$

The length of $A´B´$ is one half the length of AB.

Sam says that any two right triangles are similar. Use a sketch in the coordinate plane to describe why this is not true.

Draw two right triangles AOB and AOC in the coordinate plane with right angle O at the origin. The legs of each triangle are drawn on the positive x-axis and positive y-axis, so the triangles both share leg AO. If the triangles are similar, then there must be a dilation that takes triangle AOB to triangle AOC, since the triangles already share right angle O. But any dilation that takes point B to point C must also take point A to point A' ≠ A, so no such dilation exists.

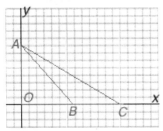

- 41 -

Find an expression to represent the height of an equilateral triangle with side length S.

Draw an equilateral triangle with side length S. From any vertex, draw the perpendicular to the opposite side. Due to the symmetry of the triangle, it does not matter which vertex is chosen. The length h of the perpendicular segment is the height of the equilateral triangle. Two congruent right triangles are formed, each with a hypotenuse of S (the sides of the original triangle), a leg of length h (the height). and a leg that is half of the side perpendicular to the height, or $0.5S$ in length. Use the Pythagorean Theorem to find an expression for h in terms of S:

$$h^2 + (0.5S)^2 = S^2$$
$$h^2 = S^2 - \frac{S^2}{4}$$
$$h^2 = \frac{3S^2}{4}$$
$$h = \frac{S\sqrt{3}}{2}$$

An expression for the height is $\frac{S\sqrt{3}}{2}$.

Find an expression that gives the distance from (a, b) to $(-a, -b)$.

The distance between points (a, b) and $(-a, -b)$ can be determined by drawing a sketch and using the Pythagorean Theorem. Draw a vertical and horizontal segment to form a right triangle with a hypotenuse equal to the length of the distance from (a, b) and $(-a, -b)$. The lengths of the legs of the triangle are given by the expressions $2a$ and $2b$. Apply the Pythagorean Theorem:

$(2b)^2 + (2a)^2 = d^2$
$4b^2 + 4a^2 = d^2$

$d = \sqrt{4(a^2 + b^2)}$
$d = 2\sqrt{a^2 + b^2}$

The distance is $2\sqrt{a^2 + b^2}$ units. This is twice the distance from the origin to the point (a, b).

A cylindrical measuring cup has a capacity of 2 cups. The cup has a height of 5 inches. If 1 cup = 14.4375 cubic inches, determine the diameter of the cup to the nearest tenth.

Use the formula for the volume of a cylinder, $V = \pi r^2 h$, to determine the radius of the measuring cup:

$V = \pi r^2 h = \pi r^2(5) = 2(14.4375)$
$r^2 = \frac{28.875}{5\pi}$

- 42 -

$r \approx 1.356$

The radius of the cup is about 1.36 inches. The diameter is twice the radius, so the diameter is about 2.7 inches, to the nearest tenth.

Determing how the equation of a linear model can help predict results beyond the data values

The equation of a linear model represents the best-fit line for the data. This means that a linear relationship is shown in the data, and the equation best gives the value of one categorical variable given the value of the other, particularly for values that fall between the data points. Since a linear equation has a domain of all real numbers, substituting a value of a variable that is beyond the data values will give a corresponding value for the other variable. The further away the value is form the given data, however, the less likely the results will be reliable. This also depends on the actual real-world situation that is being described by the data.

Sum of two rational numbers must be rational by adding and simplifying the sum $\frac{a}{b} + \frac{c}{d}$

A rational number is a ratio of two integers, such as $\frac{2}{3}$. In general, the expressions $\frac{a}{b}$ and $\frac{c}{d}$ represent any two rational numbers, provided that both b and d are not zero. Add the expressions using a common denominator:

$$\frac{a}{b} + \frac{c}{d} = \frac{ad}{db} + \frac{cb}{db} = \frac{ad + cb}{db}$$

The product of two integers results in an integer. Also, the sum of two integers results in an integer. Therefore, the expression $\frac{ad+cb}{db}$ is a ratio of two integers. This means that the sum of any two rational numbers is also rational.

Wendy claims that the irrational number $\sqrt{24}$ is approximately equal to the rational number 12. Find her error.

Wendy most likely made the mistake of thinking a square root of a number is about one half of the number. In general, this is not true. The square root of a number is the number that when squared, or multiplied by itself, gives the original number. To approximate the irrational number $\sqrt{24}$, Wendy should consider perfect squares that are close to 24. The perfect square $25 = 5^2$ is very close to 24, so 5 would be a better approximation for $\sqrt{24}$. Since 24 is a little less than 25, $\sqrt{24}$ is little less than 5. A calculator shows that $4.9^2 = 24.01$.

What is the reciprocal of the number -8^{-6}? Use another expression with an integer exponent.

The reciprocal of a nonzero number a can be written as $\frac{1}{a} = a^{-1}$. Apply this formula to the number -8^{-6}.

$$\frac{1}{-8^{-6}} = (-8^{-6})^{-1}$$

$= (-1 \cdot 8^{-6})^{-1}$ Rewrite -8^{-6} as $-1 \cdot 8^{-6}$.
$= (-1)^{-1}(8^{-6})^{-1}$ Apply the property $(ab)^n = a^n b^n$.
$= -1 \cdot 8^6$ Apply the property $(a^m)^n = a^{mn}$.
$= -8^6$ Multiply.

The reciprocal of -8^{-6} is -8^6. Note that the reciprocal of a number retains the sign of the number, and that the product of a number and its reciprocal is 1.

How to cube a number written in scientific notation

A number is written in scientific notation when it has the form $a \times 10^n$, where $1 \le a < 10$ and n is an integer. To cube such a number, raise it to the power of 3:
$(a \times 10^n)^3 = (a \times 10^n)(a \times 10^n)(a \times 10^n)$

By the commutative property of multiplication, the factors in the product can be rearranged so that powers of 10 are together:
$(a \times 10^n)(a \times 10^n)(a \times 10^n) = (a \cdot a \cdot a)(10^n \cdot 10^n \cdot 10^n) = a^3 \times 10^{3n}$

This shows that to cube a number of the form $a \times 10^n$, cube the number a and multiply the exponent on the power of 10 by 3. If the number must be written in scientific notation, check that
$1 \le a^3 < 10$.

Characteristics of the graph of any proportional relationship

A proportional relationship is represented by the equation $y = kx$, where k is a nonzero constant. When $x = 0$, $y = 0$; therefore, the graph of any proportional relationship is a straight line through the origin. The slope of the line is k. The line cannot be a vertical line, since the equation of a vertical line through the origin is $x = 0$, which is not a proportional relationship and is also not a function. The line also cannot be a horizontal line, because it is assumed the value of k is nonzero.

Josie solves a one variable linear equation, and arrives at the equation 4 = 4. She concludes the solution is x = 4. Find her mistake.

Josie arrived at an equation that is not dependent on the value of x. This is because the equation 4 = 4 does not have any variables in it. She also arrived at a true statement, which means no matter what value the variable x takes on, the equation will be true. This means that the complete solution to the equation is *all real numbers*. There are therefore an infinite number of solutions to the equation. Had Josie arrived at a false equation, such as 3 = 4, then the equation would have no solution.

Clearing out decimals to get integer coefficients when solving a one variable linear equation

To clear out decimals to get integer coefficients when solving a one variable linear equation, multiply both sides of the equation by the appropriate power of 10. The power is determined by counting the greatest number of digits after the decimal point for all of the coefficients. For example, in the equation $2.4x - 3.2 = 1.5x$, multiply by 10 to get the coefficients 24, 32, and 15. If the equation was $0.24x - 3.2 = 1.5x$, multiply by 100 to get the coefficients 24, 320, and 150. This procedure can help solve an equation with decimal coefficients by eliminating having to add and subtract decimal coefficients of like terms.

What is the solution of the system $x + y = 3$ and $2y + 2x = 6$?

Solving the first equation for x gives $y = 3 - x$. Substitute this expression into the 2nd equation:
$2y + 2x = 6$
$2(3 - x) + 2x = 6$
$6 - 2x + 2x = 6$
$6 = 6$

The solution leads to a true equation that is independent of the variables. This means that there are infinitely many solutions. The two original equations are actually the same; multiplying the first equation by 2 results in the 2nd equation. Therefore any point (x, y) such that $x + y = 3$ is a solution to the system.

Using a system to determine if the sum of two numbers equal the difference of the two numbers

Let both the sum and difference of the two numbers be N. If the two numbers are x and y, write the system as follows:
$x + y = N$
$x - y = N$

Adding these equations together results in the equation $2x = 2N$, so $x = N$. Substituting $x = N$ into either of the equations gives $y = 0$. This means that for two numbers to have the same sum and difference, one of the numbers must be equal to that sum or difference, and the other number is equal to zero. The solution could be written as an ordered pair as $(N, 0)$, as long as the difference is calculated as $x - y$ and not $y - x$.

What is the slope and y-intercept of the graph represented by the linear equation $-3y + 4 = 5x$?

The slope and y-intercept of the graph represented by the linear equation $-3y + 4 = 5x$ can most easily be found by rewriting the equation in the form $y = mx + b$. When written in this slope-intercept form, m is the slope and b is the y-intercept. Solve the equation for y:
$$-3y + 4 = 5x$$
$$-3y = 5x - 4$$
$$y = -\frac{5}{3}x + \frac{4}{3}$$

The slope of the graph is $-\frac{5}{3}$ and the y-intercept is $\frac{4}{3}$. Note that the coefficient of x in a linear equation is the slope only when the equation is solved for y. Similarly, the constant term is the y-intercept only when the equation is solved for y.

A coupon entitles the bearer to 15% off the price of lunch. Construct a function to give the new price p of lunch given the original price x.

The new price of lunch is 15% less than the original price. To find 15% of a number, multiply by 0.15. Since x represents the original price of lunch, the expression 0.15x represents 15% of the original price. The word "off" implies subtraction, that is the 15% discount is subtracted from the original price x. Therefore the new price is $x - 0.15x = 0.85x$. The function p = 0.85x gives the new price p based on the original price x. The 0.85 represents 85%, which is the percent of the original price that is being paid.

Describe two different transformations that take the vertex $F(3, -1)$ of rectangle $FGHJ$ to $F'(1, 3)$.

There are rotations, translations, and reflections that could take vertex $F(3, -1)$ of rectangle $FGHJ$ to $F'(1, 3)$. To determine the translation, subtract coordinates: $1 - 3 = -2$ and $3 - (-1) = 4$, so translating the square 2 units left and 4 units up works. Also, a sketch of the points shows that a rotation of 90° counterclockwise about the origin of vertex $F(3, -1)$ results in the image $F'(1, 3)$. This can be verified by checking the segment from the origin to F is perpendicular to the segment from the origin to F'.

Triangle ABC is isosceles. The exterior angle at vertex B has a measure of 88°. Find the measures of the angles of the triangle.

Triangle ABC is isosceles, which means that two sides are congruent. It also means that the two base angles have the same measure. The exterior angle measure at vertex B is 88°, so the measure of angle B is $180° - 88° = 92°$. If angle B were one of the base angles, then the sum of the base angles would be $92° + 92° = 184°$. This is impossible, since the sum of the angle measures of a triangle is 180°. The measures of the base angles have a sum of 88°, so each has a measure of 44°. The angle measures are 44°, 44°, and 92°.

Solving how the diameter of a sphere can be determined given its volume

The formula for the volume of a sphere is $V = \frac{4}{3}\pi r^3$, where r is the radius of the sphere. If the volume is known, then the value can be substituted into the formula. Then the equation can be solved for r as follows:

$$V = \frac{4}{3}\pi r^3$$
$$3V = 4\pi r^3$$
$$\frac{3V}{4\pi} = r^3$$
$$r = \sqrt[3]{\frac{3V}{4\pi}}$$

A calculator can be used to get an approximate value of r if needed. Finally, the diameter of the sphere is twice the radius, so multiply this value by 2 to get the diameter of the sphere.

Reading

Literature

Explicit information

Explicit information is the information that is found in a passage or story. This information can include facts, descriptions, and statements about the characters, setting, or events in a story. Explicit information is not suggested or hinted at; it is definite because it is stated right in the passage. Explicit information takes many shapes; in a description it might be that "Tom was taller than his brother." In dialogue it could be, "I have never been to Texas before." Or it could be found in an event: "Charles hit his head on the bottom of the swimming pool." Explicit information is often used as supporting evidence when making an inference.

Identify the explicit information in the following excerpt.

> Bernard loved to paint. He regularly worked eight hours a day, six days a week, perfecting his craft. His sister Julie was an actress. On days when she was performing or rehearsing, she put in very long hours. Sometimes she worked 14 or 16 hours a day.

Explicit information is information which is found within the text itself. It is not suggested in any way. This excerpt tells about a brother and sister and what they did. It tells us that Bernard loved to paint and worked on his painting eight hours a day. It also says that his sister Julie was an actress and that he sometimes rehearsed 14 or 16 hours a day. This information is all explicit. It is stated in the excerpt. The reader does not need to make an inference or guess at anything. Everything is factual. When you read, think about the information in the story and whether it is explicit or not.

Inference

An *inference* is basically a good guess that a reader makes using the explicit information that is in a passage or story. An inference can also be based on personal experience combined with the information in a passage. For instance, a story may say that several people are leaving a movie theater and many of them are crying. The logical conclusion, both from the explicit information and personal knowledge, is that the movie was sad. A good inference is supported by the information in a passage. Inferences are different from explicit information: they are not clearly stated in a passage, only hinted at. The reader must determine—or *infer*—for himself what the author is suggesting. A good reader puts the clues together to produce a conclusion that is both logical and likely to be true.

Read the following excerpt and decide why Alex did not want to see the puppy.

> Dr. Thomas walked up to Alex in the waiting room. He spoke as gently as he could. "I'm sorry about Rover. We did everything we could to save him. But he was just too sick. I know how much you loved him. But I have something to show you." Then Dr. Thomas showed Alex a cute little puppy. "No," the boy shouted. "I don't want to see your dog."

You can infer that Alex did not want to see the puppy because he was too upset about his own dog. This conclusion might be based both on what the passage says and from personal experience. In the excerpt, Dr. Thomas tells Alex that they could not save his dog. From personal experience you might realize how upsetting it is to lose a pet. That would help you come to the conclusion that Alex was grieving and didn't want to see another dog at that moment. An inference is based on the information in a passage and a reader's experience, but it is not stated in the text.

Determining the theme of a story

The *theme* of a story is the lesson that it teaches. It is what the reader learns from what happens in a story. The theme is linked to the characters, the setting, and the events in a story. The theme develops with the development of the plot. Some themes are fairly common. These themes are called *universal themes*; they suggest things about life, society, and human nature. Themes are an important part of literature because they serve the purpose of teaching the reader or listener a truth about life. The theme is developed by how a character or characters respond to their situations and challenges.

Tell why the theme of the following excerpt should be "Overconfidence can lead to a fall."

> Bella was happy. She auditioned for the starring role in the school play and she felt sure she'd got the part. Afterwards, she told her friends she would be starring in the play. But on Tuesday when the director said they had offered the part to Sara Goodwin, she started crying.

The excerpt tells the story of a girl who has an audition and thinks she got the starring role. She is so confident that she even tells her friends that she has the part. But then she learns that the role was offered to someone else and she starts to cry. She was overly confident about her success and was subsequently devastated when she learned of her failure, and that is the lesson of the story. If you are overly confident you may have a fall. That is the theme of the story. A theme is the lesson that a story teaches. This particular theme is found often in literature. A theme is not stated in a passage: the reader must deduce it from the plot of the story.

Objective summary

An *objective summary* of a story has several components. It should include the main idea of the story, the most important details or events that occur, and the main characters and what happens to them. A summary is not a general statement about what a story is about, nor is it a paraphrase. Paraphrases retell a story and give too much information about what happens, including some that is not important; summaries do not. A summary will not include everything in the story. In order to write an objective summary, you will need to think about what happens in the story. You will need to decide what it is mostly about and what details are the most important. Objective summaries do not include personal feelings or opinions.

Read the summary and discuss how it could be improved.

> This story is about a man and a woman who moved to the West many years ago. There was a lot of information about covered wagons or "prairie schooners," as they called them. I liked the story because of that.

The summary tells the main idea of the story, but it doesn't include the details of what happens in the story. It does not include the main characters and what they did or what challenges they faced. It does not summarize the plot. Another problem with the summary is that it is not objective; it is subjective. The writer describes what he thinks about the story. But personal opinions have no place in an objective summary of a story. To improve it, the writer should remove his personal opinion and add descriptions of who was in the story, what important things happened to them, and how the story ended.

Driving the action

There are many ways in which the action of a story may be driven. Dialogue is one of them. What a character says either to another character or about a situation may propel the action by revealing what a character is thinking or what he may do. Similarly, what a character says will tell the audience what he is like. His manner of speaking, what he says, and how he says it are all clues to his personality. Dialogue can also provoke a decision by showing what the character intends to do in the future. Incidents in a story also propel the action because the plot is made up of events that build on events. Incidents such as a confrontation could reveal aspects of a character or provoke a decision.

Read the excerpt and tell how it reveals aspects of the speaker.

> I told you I wasn't ever going to become a doctor and yet here you are bringing the topic up again. I think I am just going to put a sign on my door that says "No Medical School." Are you going to harangue me all day?

The person who is speaking sounds very sure of what he does not want to do and is forcefully resisting any attempt by someone else, a person not revealed, to try to get him to go to medical school. The speaker's character is resolute and somewhat dramatic because he plans to put a sign on his door to remind the unnamed person that he has no intention of doing what the other person wants. It could be a parent, a wife or even a friend who is urging this action. The character also seems somewhat young because he seems to have to defend his decision so strongly.

Read the excerpt and tell how this incident propels the action of the story and provokes a decision.

> It was a perfect day it seemed, until Sam saw the thunderheads roll in. He knew that it would be dangerous to be in a rowboat in the middle of the lake during a thunder and lightning storm. Suddenly the sky became darker and he heard a clap of thunder.

This incident certainly propels the action of the story. It would appear that Sam is in a rowboat in the middle of the lake having a lovely time when he hears a clap of thunder. He realizes that a lake is a dangerous place to be so this event means that Sam must take action. What that action is would be of interest to the reader because it will help form the plot of the story. The incident also forces Sam to make a decision about what he should do. This will help the reader better understand Sam as a character.

Context clues

Context clues are one of the best tools in understanding the meaning of unknown words or phrases. The sentence that contains the word or phrase and the sentences before and after the unknown word or phrase often have clues that suggest the meaning. When attempting to understand what a word or phrase means, try to think of a synonym and then replace the unknown word with the synonym to see if it makes sense in the sentence. Many words have more than one meaning, so it is only the context that will tell the reader what is meant. For instance, the word "bluff" can mean a trick or a kind of hill. In the sentence "He stood on a bluff overlooking the ocean," the context is clear. In this instance it means a type of hill.

Read the following sentences and tell how to understand the meaning of "sedentary."

> I like my job typing medical records except for one thing. I find it very sedentary. I would rather have a job where I can move around more.

"Sedentary" means "inactive" or "deskbound." When you read the excerpt you can determine the meaning from the context clues. The selection tells you that the author likes his job except for one thing and that he would rather have a job that allowed him to move around more. This clue helps you understand what "sedentary" means. If you insert the synonyms "inactive" or "deskbound" in place of "sedentary," you can see that the excerpt makes sense. Context clues help you understand the meanings of unknown words. Context clues are hints as to the meaning of a word or phrase.

Figurative language

Figurative language is the use of words and expressions to expand reality in a vivid way. It is the use of language in a non-literal way, which means using language in a non-traditional manner in order to create an image. It is often used by poets. Examples of figurative language include simile, metaphor, personification, hyperbole, onomatopoeia and alliteration. *Similes* compare things using the words "like" or "as," for example, "She is as gentle as a lamb." *Metaphors* compare things without using comparing words: "She is a lamb when dealing with others." *Personification* gives a thing or animal human traits: "The ocean spoke of foreign places and dreams." *Hyperbole* is an exaggeration that is vivid but not believable: "She is the kindest person in the world." *Onomatopoeia* is when words sound like what they are, such as "hiss, hiss" to describe the sound a snake makes. *Alliteration* is the use of consecutive words that start with the same letter: "Raining, ripping, racing, running..."

Read the excerpt and tell what form of figurative language the phrase "come down like a sluggish sea" is and why.

> The weather changed. The air had come down like a sluggish sea, weighing us down with its heavy pressure.

The phrase, "air had come down like a sluggish sea" is an example of a simile. Similes add depth to writing and make it richer. They are used to create a more vivid image of

- 50 -

something in the reader's mind. In this case, the air coming down "like a sluggish sea" means the air is very heavy. The phrase is not a metaphor because it compares to things using a comparison word, in this case "like." It can't be hyperbole as there is no exaggeration in the phrase. It is not an example of personification or onomatopoeia either, although there is a hint of alliteration in the phrase.

Denotative vs. connotative meaning of words

Words often have both a denotative meaning and a connotative meaning. The *denotative meaning* is the dictionary definition of a word. The *connotative meaning* is the associations that a word carries with it, associations above and beyond its literal meaning. For instance, the word "decorative" is a synonym for "fancy," but so is the word "extravagant." Yet "extravagant" has a rather negative meaning where "decorative" does not. "Extravagant" suggests something that is overdone or excessive. Readers should recognize the connotative meanings that writers include in their stories in order to better understand the writers' intent.

Read the following sentence and explain the connotative meanings of "strong-willed" and how it compares to "pig-headed."

> Some people admired Uncle Fred because they thought he was strong-willed, but others considered him pig-headed.

Both the words "strong-willed" and "pig-headed" have the literal or denotative meaning of "stubborn." The word "pig-headed," however, also has a rather negative connotation of being so stubborn to the point of being stupid and that people are frustrated by such a person, while "strong-willed" has a more positive meaning of being stubborn as a good characteristic. The connotations that a word add to a sentence will influence how the reader interprets a story's characters and events. That is why it is important to notice which words the writer chooses to use. In this instance, the writer has drawn a contrast between positive and negative.

Read the excerpt and tell how the analogy impacts the tone of the story.

> Clara nestled underneath a tree, with her book, much in the same way that Alice of Wonderland fame might have done. Then, just like Alice, she fell asleep.

The words that a writer uses to tell a story are important because they can evoke a strong reaction in a reader. Here the writer makes an analogy to "Alice in Wonderland" in the way he describes Clara nestled under a tree with a book. The story of "Alice in Wonderland" is well known, and by making a reference to it, the writer creates a mood of mystery and tension about what may happen. The reader finds himself wondering if Clara will encounter some of the characters that Alice did when she says that Clara fell asleep. When reading, make sure to be aware of any analogy or references that the author makes to other texts to better comprehend what the author is suggesting.

Comparing and contrasting the structure of a poem to a short story

Poems have many structures. There are sonnets, haiku, and even pattern poems that take the shape of the focus of the poem. Poetry has developed over many years and its structure can be strict or, in the case of free verse, without rules. Generally a sonnet is a 14-line structure with a specific rhyming pattern and meter. Sonnets have been popular for a very long time and were a specialty of William Shakespeare. Haiku is a Japanese form of poetry that features three lines of five, seven, and five syllables, respectively. There are no strictures that are similar in a short story. Stories follow the order of the plot: the beginning, middle and end. But even that is not always the case with modern fiction, which may lack a real beginning or a definite end. Again the structure plays into the meaning and style of the poem or story by signaling to the reader the intent.

Dramatic irony

Dramatic irony is a situation when a character makes a remark about doing something that seems harmless in its context, but that the audience has more information about and realizes it could result in something unpleasant. This difference in knowledge can create suspense or humor depending on the circumstances. For instance, if a character says, "I will have a cup of tea now," and the audience knows that there is poison in the tea, it creates a situation that is suspenseful. That is an example of dramatic irony. The word "irony" comes from the Greek word for "dissembling" and it was used to describe what the Greeks thought was the gap between appearance and reality.

Transforming a story to a live performance

When transforming a story or drama to a live performance, either on stage or in film, a director will need to make decisions on how to present the story. Certainly the experience of seeing a performance of a story or drama is different because actors are speaking the dialogue or lines and are bringing the words and characters to life. But many directors choose to change the dialogue to simplify or emphasize a certain aspect of the play or film. Another decision that might be made in a staged performance is how the characters act; they may do something differently from what a person might imagine when reading a script. Yet another factor that might be different is the time period in which the action takes place. In particular, in both filmed and staged versions of Shakespearean plays, directors sometimes choose to bring the action into a modern world rather than keep it set in the time of the Renaissance.

How a filmed production of the story of Snow White might be different from the written story

In a filmed production of Snow White, you would see Snow White as a person who has certain traits that might be different from the written character. Also the evil stepmother might be better rendered and the reasons that she hated Snow White might be made clearer. Some directors might make the evil queen justified in her hatred of Snow White. For instance, a television series called "Once Upon a Time" presents these fairy tale characters in ways very different from the popular perception of them, giving reasons for their actions that were not included in the famous story.

How a modern fiction draws from the past

There is an old saying that writers like to quote: "there's nothing new under the sun." And to a large extent this is true because many of the modern stories, themes, patterns of events, and character types are taken from traditional stories, myths or religious works and then changed to make them seem new. For instance, the film "Wrath of the Titans," which is a sequel takes up where its predecessor, "Clash of the Titans," ended. These films are based on the myth of the ancient Greek hero Perseus and the tale of his life, which most people do not know. But that fact is unimportant because the movie makes the plot readily available to them. Mainstream actors give these mythic characters life, and the movies are filled with action to excite the audience by bringing an ancient tale to life while using the most advanced technology to create special effects. While the story is from myth, the director makes it current in that the actors bring color and personality to the mythic people they play.

Importance of being able to read and comprehend a wide variety of texts by the end of grade 8

It is vital that, by the time a student completes grade 8, he or she will be able to read and comprehend literature, including stories, dramas, and poetry, at the grade 8 level. Students need that level of comprehension in order to have a basis for furthering their ability to read and experience the many great classics of literature that are at that level. It will also build a foundation for the student to read even more difficult texts as he or she enters high school. The ability to read and comprehend literature will lead to a student having a sound background in the cultural aspect of literature and will give the student an excellent background and preparation for whatever the student wishes to pursue in his or her life. It is also an excellent aid to learning more vocabulary.

Informational Texts

Finding textual evidence

Explicit information is information that is stated in a text. It is not something that is hinted at. A nonfiction text is usually made up of a main idea and supporting details. These supporting details are explicit: they are stated right in the text. They can be used to support an inference that is not stated in the text, or to support the main claims of an essay. Supporting information should be based on fact, not opinion. It should come from a reliable source and be something that others can verify. When trying to find textual evidence for what a text says explicitly, you will need to look for details that give more information about it.

Read the following excerpt and identify which information is explicit.

> In ancient times the value of an ox was the basis for the monetary systems of the Greeks, Assyrians, Mesopotamians, and the Egyptians. Each of these territories had their own currency. For instance, Egypt traded in gold and Greece in silver or copper.

All of the information in the excerpt is explicit. Nothing is hinted at. It says that the value of an ox was the basis for the monetary system for ancient Greeks, Assyrians, Mesopotamians, and the Egyptians. It adds that each of these territories had their own currency. It further informs that Egypt traded in gold and Greece in silver or copper. All of this information is factual. There are no opinions in the excerpt. There is nothing with which to make an inference. The details support the main idea that the ancients had monetary systems. All of the information can be checked to see if it is accurate.

Inference

An inference is a best guess. It is a conclusion that a reader can make from the information in a passage. For instance, if a passage says that a man is running down the street holding a woman's handbag, and there is a woman yelling for help in the distance, someone watching the scene might come up with the conclusion that the man is a thief and has stolen the woman's handbag. It could be an incorrect conclusion, but based on the evidence in the passage, it is the best guess that can be made. When you make an inference, you need to be able to tell what textual evidence supports the conclusion or inference. In this case, the fact that a man is running away holding a woman's handbag and a woman is yelling for help leads you to the conclusion.

Identify which information in the excerpt supports the inference that plants need more water when it is hot than when it is cool.

> *Sweat is water that evaporates on the skin. Sweating is a process which cools the body. People sweat more in hot weather. Similarly, plants are cooled by evaporating water. Most of the water a plant takes in is used to keep it cool.*

The information that supports the inference that plants need more water when it is hot then when it is cool is that plants are like people. The excerpt says that plants are cooled by evaporating water. The excerpt also says that people sweat more in hot weather, so the reader can determine from this evidence that plants need more water when it is hot than when it is cool. The inference that is made is based on the explicit information in the excerpt. An inference is the best conclusion that you can make based on the information you have.

Determining the main idea of a passage

The main idea of a passage is what the passage is mostly about. It is the main point of the passage. Sometimes the main idea is stated in a passage by the use of a topic sentence either at the beginning of the passage or elsewhere. Sometimes the main idea may be found in the title of the passage. Oftentimes the main idea is not stated in the passage; the reader needs to determine it from the information or details in the passage. The main idea will become more and more obvious to a reader as detail after detail supports it. Some information in the passage may not be supporting, but most ideas and details will support the main idea. The main idea is filled out by the supporting details in a passage.

Decide what the main idea of the following excerpt is, "There are many processes in making coins."

> The United States Mint makes our money. The government chooses the designs. Artists make a clay model, and then they create a plaster model. A steel mold is made from this plaster model. A metal alloy is used for the coins. One machine punches out the coin and another imprints it with the design.

The information in the excerpt deals with the processes of making coins. It details what happens first, second, third, and so on when making a coin. The main idea is not stated in the excerpt, so the reader needs to put the details together to determine what it is. All of the details support the main idea being, "There are many process in making coins." All of the details describe these processes. The details about how coins are made are explicit: they are facts that can be checked. The central idea emerges from these facts and is shaped by the details that tell about the coin making processes. This is what supporting details do. They shape or tell more about the main idea so that the reader can tell what a passage is mostly about.

Objective summary

An objective summary of an informational text tells what the main idea of the text is and includes the important details. It tells what the text is mostly about and includes the most important supporting details. A summary should not include too much information; it is not a paraphrase of the information. It is important to select only the most important details to include. A summary should also be objective. This is achieved by focusing on the main idea rather than any opinions that might be in the text but that are not related to the main idea. It would also not include any personal opinions on the subject.

Read the summary and explain how to improve it.

> Edgar Degas was a great artist who broke with tradition and became an Impressionist. His paintings and sculptures are included in the collections of major museums everywhere. In his forties, his vision became poor and he worked more on sculptures because he could feel them. He died in 1917 at the age of 83. His father was a banker.

This summary is quite good. It has a main idea and includes some of the important details. The main idea is that Degas was a great artist. Supporting details include that his paintings and sculpture are included in collections of major museums as well as the fact that he had poor vision and turned to sculpting because he could feel the sculptures. While the information about his death is not perhaps the most important, it is of interest that he lived to the age of 83. The one glaring error with the summary is that it mentions the fact that his father was a banker. This does not directly relate to the main idea. It is not a supporting detail and is unimportant to the central thesis of the passage. It should be deleted.

Techniques used by authors

There are various techniques that authors use to make connections among and distinctions between individuals, ideas, or events. An author may choose to compare and contrast individuals, ideas, or events. This allows the reader to quickly see how something or someone is similar to or different from another thing or person. A second technique is through the use of analogies. An author may liken an idea, individual, or events by using analogies to show how they are similar and make her point clearer. An author might also put individuals, ideas, or events into categories to show how they are linked.

Read the excerpt and tell how the author makes connections between ideas.

On the exterior it looked tidy and pleasant—a little log cabin with a fence around it. The lawn was cut close and the bushes were all tended to. No weeds in this yard. Inside was another story. The furniture was covered with dust. Huge spider webs dangled from the ceiling, and the floor was covered with dirt.

The author is comparing and contrasting the outside of a cabin with the inside. This is how the ideas are connected. Although the exterior looked tidy and pleasant, the interior was completely the opposite. It was dusty and dirty and had not been cleaned in a long time. Writers often link ideas. When a compare-and-contrast connection is made, the reader is quick to see the similarities and the differences between the two ideas or people being compared. Other ways to connect ideas is through categorizing. This technique is often used in scientific texts. Analogy is another way to connect ideas. This shows the relationship between two things or people so it is clearer to a reader.

Context clues

Context clues are an important resource when it comes to understanding the meaning of unknown words and phrases. Hints to the meaning of a word or phrase may be found in either the sentence in which the word or phrase is used or the sentences immediately before and after it. When determined the meaning of the word or phrase, substitute the synonym that you have for the unknown word or phrase. If it is still understandable, it is likely you have determining the meaning of the word. Figurative usage can also often be determined from the context of the text. Sometimes when reading technical text, it may be necessary to read more of the document to determine the meaning of a word.

Determine the meaning of "cordial" in the following excerpt.

The salesperson smiled when the couple came into the store. She told them to take their time in choosing a ring. She chatted with them about their future plans. She was the most cordial salesperson they had ever met.

The excerpt states that the salesperson smiled. It says that she told them to take their time and that she chatted with them. Obviously the word "cordial" has a positive meaning based on these context clues. They seem to like the salesperson. She seems very pleasant. If you put the word "pleasant" in place of "cordial," the sentences make sense. Through this process it is possible to use context clues to help the reader understand the meaning of an unknown word. The same process can be used to decipher the meanings of unknown expressions or sayings.

Determine the meaning of "sense of foreboding."

All day long Ron kept thinking about Sue. For some unknown reason he was worried about her. He had a strong sense of foreboding that something was about to go wrong in Sue's city. His fear was well-founded. Early the next morning, there was an earthquake. But fortunately, it was mild. Sue was shaken but unharmed.

The passage says that Ron kept thinking about Sue and that he was worried about her. Then it says that his fear was well-founded because there was an earthquake. From this the reader can determine what a "sense of foreboding" means. It means having a feeling that something bad will happen. If you substitute that phrase for "sense of foreboding," it makes sense. This process helps you understand what a word or phrase means. Always check for clues in the sentence and surrounding sentences to determine the meaning of unknown words or phrases.

Read the excerpt and determine the meaning of "contusion."

> Eli had fallen off the swing and his mother was very upset when she saw the swelling on his forehead. She rushed him to the emergency room. Dr. Vargas examined Eli and told his mother that it was just a contusion and nothing to worry about.

In this passage, the word "contusion" is a technical term. The reader can tell that it is a medical term because the doctor tells Eli's mother that is what he has. By reading through the passage, the reader will notice certain context clues that will help to determine the meaning of the word. Eli's mother saw a swelling on the child's head and took him to the emergency room. After the doctor examined the boy, she said the mother had nothing to worry about. The word "swelling" is key here. It suggests that "contusion" means a bump. If you replace "contusion" with "bump," the passage makes sense.

Figurative language

Figurative language is the use of ordinary words in a non-literal way or non-traditional manner. Figurative language is used by writers to expand their vision by creating images to make their writing more vivid and fresh. The literal meaning of a word or phrase is changed from its literal meaning to a figurative one. There are many different kinds of figurative language. A *simile* compares two things using the words "as" or "like." For example, "She was as clever as a fox." A *metaphor* compares two things without using the comparing words: "He was a fox when it came to getting out of a bad situation." *Personification* gives a thing or animal human traits. For example, "The fox cried out to him." When reading, look for non-traditional ways of using language that will contain hints to the meaning of the passage.

Which figurative language is used in the excerpt?

> We stood on the edge of the beach, a browned desert that offered no safe refuge, and watched the faltering ship struggling in the sea.

This is an example of a metaphor. The beach is likened to a browned desert that offered no safe refuge. They are compared without the use of the comparison words "as" or "like," so it is not a simile. The metaphor paints the beach in a negative way because it is compared to a desert with no safe refuge. The image adds vividness to the writing that would not exist if this image had not been added; it tells the reader what the author thinks of what is happening. It also suggests that something terrible is happening to the ship.

Denotative vs. connotative meaning of words

The *denotative meaning* of a word is the meaning that is found in a dictionary. It is the literal definition of a word. The connotative meaning is somewhat more subtle; it may also be listed in a dictionary, but after the literal meaning. The *connotative meaning* is what is suggested by or hinted at by a word, but not stated outright. The connotative meaning

- 57 -

comes from the usage of the word. Its hidden meaning has come from personal experience. For instance, the words "lovely" and "exquisite" both mean "attractive," but "exquisite" suggests someone who is gorgeous or perfect-looking while "lovely" is less strong. When reading texts, you should always pay attention to words that have strong connotations because these words are a key to the author's opinion or point of view.

Read the following and explain the connotative meaning of the word "chef" and how it compares to "cook."

I have always thought of myself as a chef, not a cook.

Both the words "chef" and "cook" can be defined as "someone who prepares food," but the word "chef" carries a higher status than "cook." It suggests someone who prepares food professionally rather than someone who merely prepares food as a necessity, such as for a family. The speaker obviously thinks highly of her cooking ability and prefers to think of herself as a professional. When you are reading, pay close attention to what a writer is suggesting through the choice of word. When you are writing, choose words carefully so that you don't depict something in a negative way by mistake. Utilize a dictionary and thesaurus to help you find the perfect word.

Analogy vs. allusion

An *analogy* is a relationship; it can be a relationship between two things, people, or even words. When reading a text, look for words that signify an analogy, such as "like" or "the same as." A writer might say that his situation is about the same as being stranded on a desert island. That becomes an image for what he feels. It helps make his frame of mind clearer. In the same way, an *allusion* will make a point clearer. Writers often allude to another circumstance or event to clarify their own experience. For instance, in the following sentence, the allusion to a fairy tale tells you what the writer is trying to say: "I'm working harder than Cinderella, but I don't see a prince in my future." The allusion to the famous fairy tale tells you that the speaker is not very happy.

Analyzing the structure of a paragraph

When reading a paragraph, a close study of the way in which is it structured is helpful. The reader should first look to see how the author begins the paragraph. Does she open the paragraph with a topic sentence or does she use some other technique, such as a humorous or dramatic statement, to begin the paragraph? If the second is true, does a topic sentence follow or do supporting details come next? If the topic sentence is at the start of the paragraph, supporting details would follow it. The last sentence is the conclusion. Some conclusions can be topic sentences, but that is not usual. The last sentence most often brings closure to the paragraph and signals the end. Paragraphs can also have an overall structure. The structures of a paragraph include: a comparison and contrast structure, a cause and effect structure, a sequential structure, or a problem and solution structure. The structure of the paragraph depends a great deal on its main idea.

Determine the structure of this paragraph.

> The starfish hunts for clams in a strange way. When a starfish finds a clam, it wraps some of its arms around the clam. Then it pulls the clam open. After this, the starfish opens its mouth and pushes its stomach out of its mouth. The stomach goes into the clam shell and eats the clam and the starfish swallows its stomach again.

The paragraph opens with a topic sentence: "The starfish hunts for clams in a strange way." This sentence tells what the paragraph will be about. The other sentences are supporting details. They tell more about the main idea. The last sentence tells what happens at the end of the process of a starfish eating a clam. It provides closure. In determining the overall structure, the reader can use an elimination process. There is nothing to compare to the clam, so it is not a compare-and-contrast structure. There is no cause and effect structure indicated, nor is there a problem-and-resolution structure. The overall structure is sequential. The paragraph tells what happens in the order that it occurs.

Determining an author's point of view

The author's point of view is not always immediately clear. It could be stated clearly in many texts, but oftentimes the author does not want the reader to know exactly how he feels so a reader needs to discover it by the choice of words that an author uses, the information he includes, and any other relevant factors. It is important to read a text closely to determine what an author thinks about an event, person, topic or issue. Always check for any emotional statements that will give an idea of what the author is feeling. Look for any judgments an author may make about his topic, and piece together what you believe is the author's point of view.

How an author should acknowledge and respond to conflicting evidence or viewpoints

When discussing a controversial subject, an author has a duty to bring up both sides of an argument. The author may feel a certain way, but should still include opposing viewpoints in order to have a seemingly objective passage or essay. An author can, of course, refute the viewpoints but would need to use logical reasons why and cite any evidence that she wishes to include as testimony. In some cases, the author may not wish to side with either position, but merely to address the issues and give conflicting evidence so that the reader can form his own opinion about an issue.

Determine the author's point of view in the excerpt.

> Although flawed in some aspects, the play certainly kept the audience's attention, and there were cheers at the end. I look forward to Clemente's next play.

Based on what the author says in the excerpt, it would appear that he liked Clemente's play, even though he acknowledges some problems with it. He says as much by saying that, in spite of being "flawed" in some ways, the audience seemed to like the play because "there were cheers at the end." Then he goes on to say that he looks forward to Clemente's next play, which is the major suggestion that he, just like the audience, enjoyed the performance. It is important to read a text closely to determine what the author's opinion is by what he says and suggests.

Determining the purpose of the text

While reading a text, you should always try to determine its purpose. To do so, ask yourself why the author wrote the text and what affect the writing has on you. Is the purpose to explain something or tell how to do something? Does the text try to persuade you of something? Perhaps the text is making an appeal to your emotions. The signs that a text is attempting to persuade you include an author offering an opinion and telling why she thinks that way. On the other hand, if a text is simply informative, it will have many facts that will give details about an event or person or a thing, but not try to persuade you of anything. Manuals that come with equipment are clearly not persuasive; they simply are instructive.

Describe the purpose of this excerpt.

> Bristlecone pines are remarkable. They are the longest-lived form of plant life in the world. These trees can live as long as 5,000 years. Some bristlecone pines standing today in the western United States were seedlings when the Egyptian pyramids were being built. They were mature trees by the year 1 AD.

The purpose of the excerpt is to inform. The way in which a reader can tell this is that the text has concrete facts and details about the bristlecone pines. It does not have any opinions, other than the obvious one, that "bristlecone pines are remarkable." The author of the excerpt is not trying to persuade the reader of anything other than that. And the details that she includes make the pines very remarkable. The formal language is to the point and the information is interesting. The writer wants people to learn about the bristlecone pines; she is not selling them nor is she asking people to protect them.

Advantages and disadvantages of using different media

There are advantages and disadvantages to using different media. Print and digital texts are portable so you can bring them with you wherever you go. That is a distinct advantage, but the disadvantages are many in comparison with video or multimedia. For instance, if you are interested in learning how to cook a certain dish, you can read a recipe, but seeing a video would be much more informative. If you are reading an autobiography of someone, then a multimedia presentation will allow you to hear recordings of a person or see an actor playing the person, and that may bring the book to life. This is the primary difference between print and performed versions.

How a movie version of Superman would be different from a comic book version

A movie version of Superman would be quite different from a comic book version because an actor would play the superhero and would speak as well as actually fly through the air. The comic book version would mean that the person would only be able to read the dialogue, not hear it. The pictures in the comic book would show what Superman is doing, but there would be no movement in the images as there would be in a movie. The movie could have special effects and special lighting to make the plot scarier or tenser, but such techniques are likely not as effective in a comic book version.

Importance of being a proficient reader of literary nonfiction texts by grade 8

It is of great importance that a student who reaches the end of grade 8 should be proficient in reading nonfiction texts because the texts that he will have to comprehend in the following years of school will be more difficult. These texts contain information on a variety of subjects that a student needs to master. Without being able to read well, a student may fall behind in his academic studies. Reading well is also the means of developing a good vocabulary. These skills will ultimately benefit the student not only in academic pursuits, but in all walks of life.

Writing

Producing clear and coherent writing

Every type of writing has its own characteristics, but to attain clear and coherent writing, it is necessary to plan what you will be writing about. You need to decide what your goal is; are you trying to write a narrative or are you writing to inform or persuade? After you have decided on your goal, you need to organize your material, especially in the case of nonfiction writing. You need to have a clear picture of your main ideas and supporting details. If you are planning to write a narrative, you need to pay attention to both developing your story in a clear and flowing manner and to creating believable characters through use of precise language including descriptions, dialogue and action. Another requirement is the establishment of a tone that is appropriate to the task, purpose, and audience. Finally, make sure your writing is grammatically correct and has no spelling errors.

Constructive criticism

You can work with your peers and adults to improve your writing. Have them read what you are writing and suggest ways to change it. An important part of the process is planning what you want to write. After you complete a first draft, you will need to revise your text. Editing the text comes next and you must develop a critical eye to make sure that the grammar and verb usage are correct and that you are using an active voice rather than a passive one. Sometimes you will find your writing fails to achieve its purpose. If that happens, you may have to start over and try something different. You may want to introduce a chart to make the material easier to understand, or change the ending to a story you are writing. Lastly, you need to learn how to assess if you have addressed your purpose and audience. Ask yourself whether the writing accomplishes what you want it to and if the language is suitable for the audience you want to reach.

Decide why the following passage needs revision and how to revise it

> Galileo was believing that the Earth moved around the Sun. They, the other teachers, did not believe that. He was sent to jail. Was being a brilliant mathematician. He was scorned by the other teachers at his university. They think him a foolish rebel. Now, we don't believe that he is considered a genius and a hero.

The writer of the passage has made a lot of grammatical mistakes. The style is not as formal as it should be and some sentences are almost incomprehensible. In the first sentence, an incorrect verb form is used. The second and fifth sentences seem to repeat the same information. The third sentence is not linked to the previous information. The fourth sentence does not have a subject. And the last sentence is a run-on. Here is one way to make those corrections:

Galileo believed that the Earth moved around the Sun. Because of this belief, he was sent to jail. Galileo was a brilliant mathematician. However, he was scorned by the other teachers at his university. In his own time, he was thought to be a foolish rebel. Now, he is considered a genius and a hero.

Now, the writing is much better organized and the mistakes are corrected.

Using the Internet

Online sources are invaluable tools. Writers can get works published at little or no cost as an e-book. There are other options available as well, such as editing and marketing services offered on many Internet sites. Some sites offer help with everything from style to grammar. Many sites can be used as credible research sources, where you find accurate and objective information for research projects and where you can compare information and ideas and how they may relate one to the other. Always cite all sources that you use from the Internet using the MLA (Modern Language Association) style as a guide. Additionally, the Internet has many sites where people can collaborate on projects. Chat rooms and topic websites are tools that allow an exchange of information as well as shared writing projects.

Conducting a short research project

When conducting a short research project to answer a question, draw up a list of keywords relating to the question. Use these words in a search engine to bring up websites that relate to the issue at hand. Use the most reliable websites for information to use in your research and be sure to keep track of the websites so that you can cite them in your text. While researching the subject, you will probably find related issues that would broaden the extent of your research project, so you may choose to come up with other keywords that would extend your research from its original scope. Make sure to draw from several sources when preparing your research paper. In that way, you can compare and contrast the information that is available.

When conducting research, your primary job is to list the kind of information you are looking for and then create a list of keywords to use for a search in multiple print and digital sources. Take extensive notes, noting the source that each bit of information comes from. Be sure to check on the reliability and credibility of each source. Journals, textbooks, magazines, and newspapers are all useful sources. Also, always verify how timely, accurate and credible your sources and information are. Dismiss any sources that seem questionable. When writing your report, you may paraphrase, but do not copy information down directly because that constitutes plagiarism. Use fresh language and attempt to rewrite the details and other information in your own language. Use the Modern Language Association (MLA) guidelines for all citations.

Analyze how the Bible is the basis of Andrew Lloyd Weber's musical Jesus Christ Superstar.

> Andrew Lloyd Weber's musical *Jesus Christ Superstar,* which dates from 1971, is loosely based on the last days of Christ's life from the Gospel and his relationship to Judas. However, many of the conversations and events included in the musical are not found in the Bible at all. *Jesus Christ Superstar* also makes use of songs and lyrics to bring the characters of Christ and Judas to life. It follows Christ's life from the time he and his disciples enter Jerusalem until the crucifixion, including Judas's betrayal of Christ. Judas is a very developed character in the musical and most of the action is the tension between Christ and him. Weber, like many other modern artists, makes use of the story

- 63 -

from the bible, but uses it in a modern way so that it is appealing to modern audiences. Some of the music from the musical is still popular today.

Terri is researching a paper on hurricanes. Evaluate the following sources as to their reliability.

http://www.nhc.noaa.gov/
http://en.wikipedia.org/wiki/
Tropical_cyclone

When doing research on the Internet, you need to be extremely careful that the website you are using to get facts and details about a subject is authorized and credible. The first source is a highly credible one. It is the National Weather Service National Hurricane Center. The information on this site would be totally credible because it is run by a component of the National Centers for Environmental Prediction (NCEP) at the Florida International University in Miami, Florida. All the information that you find there is accurate and credible because it is run by scientists in that field. The second source is not so credible. Wikipedia is not considered a credible source. It is not supervised in the way that a professional encyclopedia is. There are many mistakes that are made in their information. No academic group would accept it as a reliable source.

Making writing a habit

It is important that students become habitual writers. The more a student writes, the more he will improve his writing. Whatever the purpose for writing, students should be able to formulate their ideas into words. Some tasks will be shorter than others and require less work. A letter to a friend may not be a long undertaking, but a report will require more effort and time, including rewriting and editing as well as proofreading the finished paper. But whether the writing assignment is short or long, students need to find a way to become communicators with the written word. This means employing proper grammar and spelling as well as varied syntax to keep the reader interested.

Persuasive text

Introducing a claim

An excellent way to introduce a claim is to present evidence of its validity in a logical manner. The same can be true of distinguishing your claim from alternate or opposing claims. Logical evidence based on valid sources will give your claim strength. Central to organizing your reasons and evidence is doing excellent research and finding evidence that is based on facts and comes from experts in the field. Then the passage should be organized so that one idea flows from another and into the next. When writing, place your claim at the top and then list the reasons and evidence that support the statement. This will help you organize your passage logically.

When you present a claim, there should be supporting evidence that is reliable. Without credible evidence or sources, your argument will be weak. The evidence needs to be reliable and relevant and should cover every point that is made. It is vitally important that you do a great deal of research to develop your evidence. While researching, have a critical eye and anticipate what readers might say; this will help you to develop your claim thoroughly. It is not enough to research a claim on the Internet because many Internet sources are not reliable. When using the Internet, look for sites that are objective. Find experts that you can quote and use proven statistics. Make sure to present your information in a logical manner so that the reader can easily understand your argument.

Evaluating arguments and claims

When reading a persuasive essay, the reader will want to analyze and evaluate an argument and claims based on the validity of the evidence that is given. Claims are often made by authors, but it is important that these claims are backed with evidence. This evidence, however, must come from valid sources in order for it to be accepted. Sources include books that are written by experts on a subject, information from studies that are accredited, and Internet sources that are trustworthy. When analyzing a source, ask yourself if the source has any evidence of being an authority on the subject at hand.

Recognize irrelevant evidence

Claims are sometimes introduced but the evidence is not relevant to the subject of the text. It may be because the evidence does not come from a credible source, or because the evidence may have little to do with the claim. When evaluating evidence, ask yourself what relationship the evidence has to a claim. For instance, if a writer says that global warming is not occurring and then cites evidence from a study that is 25 years old, it is probably outdated and irrelevant to the claim. The reader should be aware of this possibility and disregard any irrelevant evidence. The reader should also be wary of any evidence that is not from a valid source.

Dealing with conflicting information

When confronted with information from two different texts that have conflicting information, the reader should decide whether the conflict is a matter of fact or interpretation. Often times, particularly in political texts, the same facts may be interpreted in different and conflicting ways. It is important for the reader to evaluate these facts and see if they are based on information that is credible. Then the reader must determine whether the various interpretations are supported by the facts. This is not always easy to do, but it is important for the reader to develop a critical eye for that very purpose.

Creating cohesion

The best way to create cohesion between claims, counterclaims and evidence is to organize your ideas and then write sentences explaining your reasons and evidence that follow your main ideas logically. Careful research will result in your argument being cohesive and easy to understand. Your claim and evidence must be clearly related to each other. Words that will indicate to the reader that the claim and evidence are related include "since," "because," "as a consequence" and "as a result." You can also utilize clauses to demonstrate a relationship between the reason and the effect. Consider the following sentence: "As a result of the following observations by scientist John Neal, more people have come to believe that a good night's sleep is necessary to being healthy." The sentence establishes causality between the reason and effect. When stating counterclaims, remember to use linking words such as "but" or "on the other hand" to indicate that an alternative claim will follow.

Maintaining a formal style

A formal style is used when writing essays, both persuasive and informative. This style helps the writer achieve objectivity and keep the language precise. Formal writing consists of complex words and sentences; sentence fragments should be avoided unless they are being used for a specific reason. The tone of the writing is serious. The third person is always used, not the first or second person. An active voice is preferred because it projects more energy than a passive voice. Contractions are not used in formal writing. Sentences should be grammatically correct, as should the spelling and punctuation. When writing, reread and edit your passage several times to improve it. Vary the kinds of sentences and make sure that your ideas follow a logical order as well.
Read the following passage and identify what style it is written in.

> About two hundred years ago, world literature was growing rapidly. At that time, publishing books became profitable because people had more free time and turned to reading for entertainment. It was, however, quite a different reading compared to previous periods when books were created only for the few and not the everyman.

The excerpt is written in a formal style. The first thing to notice is that the third person is used for the viewpoint. The piece also has a serious tone and uses precise language. The sentences are complex and varied and no contractions are used. All of these details point to a formal style. If it were an informal style, the first or second person would be used, the tone would be more casual, and the language would be more generalized than is evident in this excerpt.

Importance of have a concluding statement

A concluding statement is important for a persuasive passage because it follows from and supports the argument that has been stated earlier in the passage. It should sum up the main points of the passage and give the reader a sense of completion and the passage a sense of closure. The purpose of the concluding sentence is to pull all aspects of the passage together and make sense of the ideas, evidence and details that have been included previously. The concluding statement should also be memorable because it will be last chance the writer has to convince the reader of his or her argument.

What kind of argument would the following sentence best conclude?

> Physical activities help you become stronger, live longer, and make you happier.

The sentence would make a good concluding sentence for a passage about the reasons why one should adopt some form of physical activity. Arguments could include the benefits of different activities and why physical activity makes a person become stronger, live longer and be happier. The sentence was probably preceded with information on how to get started with a physical activity, such as being sure to check with a doctor before starting a new regimen, where a person can learn more about various forms of activities, and how to decide which activity is right for the reader. This sentence would provide closure for a passage of this type.

Informational or Explanatory Text

Introducing a topic

An informational or explanatory text should have an introduction to the topic that the text will feature. One way you can accomplish this is by using a topic sentence followed by details that support your thesis. Another tactic is to use a reference to a current event, even if your topic refers to something in history. Ideas should be organized in a logical manner, with supporting details coming after a main concept. Connections can be made between concepts by using connecting words such as "however," "since," and "as a result." Distinctions between ideas should also be made clear and can be signaled by words such as "but" or "on the other hand." Other organizational tips include choosing whether to include a specific relationship such as cause and effect, question and answer, or problem and solution.

Organizing ideas

There are many ways to present information so that it is easier to understand. One effective tool is headings. Each heading introduces a new concept or idea in a text and allows the reader to see, just by skimming, what the article is about and which points are being covered. Another useful tool is graphics. Graphics are extremely useful because they present a lot of detailed information in a visual form that is easy to understand. Instead of putting the information in a paragraph where it can be lost to the reader, it can be put into a graphic such as a chart or table that will make it much more approachable. Multimedia such as voice-over, videos or even movies are other excellent ways to present information; in this modern world, people respond very easily to this kind of presentation. Difficult material can be made much more enjoyable through the use of these tools.

Developing a topic

When developing a topic in an informational or explanatory text, it is vital that the text utilizes relevant facts that clearly support the main topic. After the introduction of the topic, claim or argument, concrete details and facts that are relevant should follow. The supporting details that are cited should be from reliable sources. At times, definitions of unfamiliar terms are appropriate. Quotations by experts in the field are also a good addition to a passage because they give credibility to the text and may make the subject more interesting to read about. The results of any research that might have been done would also be of interest. Examples or anecdotal incidents will also make a text more approachable.

Creating cohesion

The use of appropriate transition words helps to clarify the relationships between ideas and concepts and creates a more cohesive passage. A good writer knows that such words and phrases serve to indicate the relationship between ideas and concepts. Words or phrases that show causality between ideas include "as a result," "consequently" and "therefore." Words that show a compare-and-contrast relationship include "however," "on the other hand," "in contrast" and "but." When introducing examples of different concepts, words such as "namely," "for example" and "for instance" act as transition words. Transition words such as "foremost," "primarily," "secondly," "former" and "latter" can be used when showing the order of importance of ideas or concepts.

Decide how the following sentences could be written so that there is a better transition between the ideas.

It was time for the whales to breed. The whales were swimming south.

The author rewriting these two sentences should first understand their relationship to one another. There is a causality suggested here. The reason that the whales were swimming south is that it was time for them to breed. To combine the sentences, you need to use an appropriate transition word. In this case there are several options. The phrase "as a result" works well because it shows the causality between the two thoughts: "It was time for the whales to breed; as a result, the whales were swimming south." Other causality words such as "consequently" or "therefore" could also be used.

Importance of using precise language and domain-specific vocabulary

Writers of informational or explanatory texts need to use precise language and domain-specific vocabulary in order to express themselves clearly. General vocabulary words are not specific enough in many cases. A formal essay relies on the use of vocabulary that shows a mastery of a topic. Besides a main idea, details need to be included that are supplied by carefully chosen, precise and domain-specific language. Some of the terms will necessitate definitions, which can be included in the essay. While researching a subject, it is important to include technical vocabulary so that it can be used during the writing of the text.

Establish and maintain a formal style

Writers of informative or explanatory passages generally use a formal style because it has a greater sense of objectivity. The use of an informal style in informative or explanatory texts is not acceptable. A formal style always uses a third person. The formal style calls for complex and varied sentences. These will add a further tone of formality and depth to the subject. The use of a formal style shows the seriousness of a topic. Formal writing also includes clear and credible supporting details. Personal opinion rarely has a place in an informative or explanatory passage unless it can be justified in some way that is supported.

Rewrite the following so it is in a formal style.

I've heard about volcanoes. I read that they are openings in the earth's surface. Lava, hot gases, and bits of rock come out of them. They are very forceful. I read that these volcanoes come from deep inside the earth.

Here is one way to re-write the passage:
Volcanoes are openings in the earth's surface from which lava, hot gases, and bits of rock erupt with great force. However, volcanoes begin deep within the earth.

Using the third person makes the passage more formal as well as more authoritative. Short and simple sentences are replaced with longer, more complex sentences, which make the passage more interesting to read. The vocabulary that is used is more sophisticated. Errors in grammar are also corrected. The final result is a text that is informed, precise and finely crafted.

Having a effective conclusion

Equally important to the beginning of an essay is an effective conclusion. A good concluding statement should review and sum up the information or explanation that precedes it in the text so that the reader can feel a sense of closure and completion. The conclusion should flow out of the information and bring the text to a logical end. Ideally the conclusion would review the most important points made in the presentation, the reasoning that is employed, and any supporting details that need to be remembered. A good conclusion should also allow the reader to reflect on what has been said, hopefully in a favorable light.

Narratives

Establishing a context

When writing a narrative, a context for the story has to be introduced; that context could consist of a description of a situation or a setting. A point of view also has to be established. It could be introduced by a narrator and may or may not be the same as the author's. The points of view can be shown through dialogue or how the narrator reacts to or describes what characters do in the story. The characters will need to be drawn very clearly through their descriptions, what they do, and what they say. The author may hide his point of view in the characters' thoughts or actions. The narrator's point of view is usually more overtly seen in what is said in the narrative by the narrator.

Decide the character and point of view in the following passage.

> Alma Way stared straight ahead. Her long delicate face was pale. Her gloved hands, clutching the hymn book, trembled as she sang. The time for her solo was near. She felt panic rising within her but she took a deep breath. Then her voice rang out, clear as a bell. The congregation nodded admiringly.

The author has chosen to tell the narrative from the third-person omniscient viewpoint, which means the narrator is all-knowing. He introduces the character of Alma Way by describing her. He tells the reader a lot about her by describing how she is staring, that her face is pale and that her gloved hands clutched a hymn book. The narrator also tells us that she feels panic. The author has drawn a thorough picture of this woman for whom he seems to have some interest in. The reader would need to read on to learn more clues about what the narrator's and author's viewpoints are.

Sequence of events

The sequence of events in a narrative should follow naturally out of the action and the plot. Rather than being forced, the sequence should follow the natural flow of a dialogue or plot and enhance what happens in the story. The only time that sequence is not in the order that events happens is when an author decides to use the literary device called flashback. In this case the action does not flow in sequence but rather jumps back and forth in time. Events in a narrative are extremely important in helping the reader understand the intent or message of a narrative, which is why it is important to take note of the way in which the plot unfolds.

Techniques used by an author

Authors employ many techniques to make their narratives come alive and have meaning. Dialogue is an important one. It is often through the dialogue that a reader learns what is happening and what a character is like or is thinking. An analysis by the reader of the dialogue can yield important information about what is happening in the narrative. Equally important are the descriptions that an author uses to help the reader visualize a setting and what a character looks or acts like. Another important technique is pacing, which sets the stage for what is happening in a plot, whether the pace is slow and then quick. The pace is the rhythm of the story and can have a strong effect on creating tension in the story,

Transitions words

Transition words are important when writing a narrative so that the reader can follow the events in a seamless manner. They can also color the plot and the characters and show the relationships between experiences and events. Sequence words such as "first," "second," and "last" assist the reader in understanding the order in which events occur, which can be important to the flow of the plot. Words such as "then" or "next" also show the order in which events occur. "After a while" and "before this" are other sequence expressions. Transition words can indicate a change from one time frame or setting to another. "We were sitting on a rock near the lake when we heard a strange sound." At this point we decided to look to see where the noise was coming from by going further into the woods." In this excerpt the phrase "as this point" signals a shift in setting. It also shows the relationship between what was happening and what came next.

Using precise language

An author's precise language can help a reader gain insight into a story that an author has written. Precise language, including phrases and sensory language, helps the reader imagine a place, situation, or person in the way that the writer wishes. The details that an author uses to describe a setting or character will help bring a story to life and convey exactly what the author envisions. Details of what characters do, the setting, and the events in a narrative help create a lively and thought-provoking story. Sensory language helps convey the mood and feeling of the setting and characters and will bring insight into the theme of a narrative. When reading, take special care to understand the range of language that an author employs in order to better comprehend the meaning.

Read the excerpt and analyze its language.

> All through his boyhood, George Willard had been in the habit of walking on Trunion Pike. He had been there on winter nights when it was covered with snow and only the moon looked down at him; he had been there in the fall when bleak winds blew and on summer evenings when the air vibrated with the song of insects.

This excerpt is filled with precise and sensory language. The descriptions of walking on Turnion Pike "when it was covered with snow and only the moon looked down," of the "bleak winds" that blew and times that "the air vibrated with the song of insects" all contribute to bring the writing to life and allowing the reader to see what the author envisions in his mind by creating images through vivid and precise language. The description of the setting uses relevant details that help the reader understand something about George Willard. The language has the effects of drawing the reader into the story and revealing more about this character.

Role of a conclusion

The conclusion of a narrative is extremely important because it shapes the entire story and creates the theme that the author was attempting to convey. The conclusion of a narrative is the resolution of the problem that is faced by the characters. Some conclusions may be tragic, such as those in the many classic tragedies; other endings may be lighthearted, much in the style of classic comedies. Modern stories tend to have endings that are more complex than the clear-cut endings of classic literature. They often leave the reader without a clear sense of how a character fares at the end. Nonetheless, this element tells the reader that life is not always clear in its conclusions, which is a lesson that many writers strive to teach.

Betsy is writing a story about a girl who wants to be on the basketball team and works out every day to get in shape. She has written about the girl's feelings and the obstacles she has had to overcome. Now she wants to find a conclusion to the story. Describe what she should look for when trying to develop a good conclusion.

Betsy should think about her character as though she were a real person because this seems to be a realistic story. She should think about what she wants to have as the story's theme. Does she want to show that hard work pays off? Or does she want to show that you cannot always get what you want even with hard work? In other words, she has to decide whether the story will have a happy ending or not. Whatever kind of an ending she decides upon, the conclusion should bring the entire story to a fitting and appropriate end so that the reader has a sense of closure. It should follow the opening and the many events that happen so that there is a form to the story.

Speaking and Listening

Discussions

Group discussions

Group discussions are useful ways to brainstorm ideas and exchange information. They can lead to interactive learning and help students develop self-confidence when speaking. It is important to read the assigned text material carefully and study it until you have a thorough understanding of it and so that you will feel comfortable when discussing it. Think about what you want to stay about the issue and practice with a friend or family member. It is useful to talk in front of a mirror so that you become comfortable with discussion of the topic. Then you will be ready for the group discussion.

Preparing for a discussion

When studying material for a discussion, be sure to make notes about any information in the material that is evidence on the topic, text, issue or ideas under discussion so that you can use it as the discussion goes on. Prepare questions that you can ask which will promote discussion rather than a single-word answer. They contribute to a fruitful discussion. Use the evidence to draw the discussion into new areas that may produce a true exchange of ideas. During the discussion, try to avoid any conflict. If conflicts arise, the discussion is likely over. A group discussion should be an exchange of ideas, not a battle of egos.

Collegial discussions

Peers should decide on the rules of a collegial discussion before it begins, and all participants should observe those rules. A reference such as *Robert's Rules of Order* is a good resource to have on hand. The goals of the discussion and the time that will be spent on each topic should also be a consensus of the participants. Leaders of the discussion should be chosen, again by a consensus, and all participants would have to honor their lead. Discussion should not be open-ended, but rather reach the goal that has been identified within the deadline. Interruptions should not be tolerated. It is also essential that all students come to the discussion well prepared. If there is disagreement, the leader(s) should mediate until a consensus can be reached and facilitate the process until voting on any key issues can begin.

A large part of the success of collegial discussions is centered on the ability of participants to pose questions that connect to the ideas that are being presented. To do this, you will need to develop the ability to connect ideas and ask good questions that will illicit even greater discussion. This can be accomplished by being prepared for the material ahead of time and mastering the relevant evidence that is available. Another skill that can be developed is the ability to make observations from what is being said.

Acknowledging new information

The exciting part of a group discussion is that different people come to it with different information and evidence. It is the duty of each participant to listen politely to everyone's point of view and the evidence that they are presenting. When new evidence is cited by a participant that may go against the direction of the discussion, the first thing to do is to recognize it and privately evaluate the evidence. If the evidence seems reliable, it is important to acknowledge this fact so that the discussion can include the new points that are being made. Many participants become unnerved by information that they did not expect, but this is exactly the goal of a group discussion: to exchange ideas in a civilized manner.

Analyzing the purpose of information presented in diverse media and formats

When presented with information in diverse media and formats such as visual displays, oral presentations and others, it is important for the listener to analyze the purpose of the display or presentation as well as the reasons that it is being included. Some presenters may have hidden reasons for including the diverse media and formats. Oftentimes political presentations make use of diverse media and formats to try to sway the listener to vote for a particular person or issue. Sometimes they have a commercial purpose in that they want the listener to purchase something. Still others may have a social purpose; they may want the listener to give back to the community, for instance. The media and formats may be extremely appealing, so the listener would do well to see what evidence, if any, is being presented with the appeal.

Analyzing a speaker's argument

The ability to analyze a speaker's argument is an important skill both as a student and an adult. The first point to examine is the objectivity of the speech and whether there are hard facts supporting what the speaker says. Examine whether the use of evidence seems logical and credible. Make an attempt to judge the quality of the evidence and how clearly that evidence is presented. A good speaker uses rhetoric to persuade the audience. However, faulty reasoning arises from evidence that is irrelevant or not credible. Ask yourself if the speaker appears dogmatic or opinionated, or if he is clearly and demonstrably open-minded.

Presentations

Presenting claims with relevant evidence and valid reasoning

A good presentation of information should have a logical flow to it. It should address all of the important points that help focus the presentation and it should be organized in a coherent manner. The claims should be followed by relevant evidence and a display of valid reasoning. It is utterly important to choose details wisely so that the audience will have the most important details without having to wade through so much information that they become lost. The sources should be both cited and current. Important points most definitely can be repeated for effect. Using graphics at appropriate times can reinforce the argument(s) you are making. It is a good idea to practice making your presentation with friends or family and listen to their critiques.

Importance of using appropriate eye contact and body language

To become an effective speaker, certain skills should be mastered. Among these skills is learning to make and maintain eye contact with the audience or other participants when appropriate. Maintaining eye contact helps assure the audience that the presentation is believable and (hopefully) enjoyable. Eye contact makes the presentation personal, as though the speaker is speaking to someone directly. Smiling at times is also crucial to making a presentation successful, as is speaking in a clear voice that can be heard but is not unnecessarily loud. The speaker should use clear diction and pronunciation as well. These skills are the hallmark of an effective presentation.

Integrating multimedia and visual displays into presentations

The world is very sophisticated technically and when an audience comes to a presentation, it is a great advantage to have multimedia and visual displays that simplify difficult material and make the material more interesting. Something as simple as a chart may enhance the main claim that you are presenting to an audience. A PowerPoint presentation would probably be even more appealing to the audience and also has the added benefit of being able to objectify everything you say. Video and audio can also add strength to your claims and evidence by bringing information to life. While these are good extras, they do not make up for a faulty oral presentation, but they can enhance it greatly.

Adapting speech to a variety of contexts

Proper English can be very elegant when spoken correctly and it is extremely important for students to learn to speak with proper grammar. Of course, the kind of language you use in a speech will depend on your audience and what you hope to achieve. When you speak, make sure your verbs are used correctly and that you are aware of the use of active and passive sentences. Active and passive verbs can be used for good effect, depending on your need. When you speak, you need to learn to vary the form of sentences you use so that you include interrogative and imperative in addition to statements. Include verbs in the conditional and subjunctive mood in your speech. Practice your speech with a friend or family member so that you can be confident when you speak.

Decide why the word "waiting" is a gerund and not a participle in the following sentence.

Waiting for the test results was the hardest part for Vicki.

"Waiting" is a gerund in the sentence. It is the subject of the sentence. A *gerund* is a form of verb that ends in *–ing* and is used in the same way that a noun is. "Waiting for the test results" is a gerund phrase. A gerund phrase contains the gerund plus any complements and modifiers. In this case, "for the test results," is a prepositional phrase. The difference between a present participle and a gerund, both of which end in *–ing*, is that a present participle is used as an adjective and a gerund is used as a noun.

Language

Function of an infinitive verb form

An *infinitive* is a verb form that is usually preceded by the word "to" and can be used as a noun, an adjective, or an adverb. When "to" is used before a verb, it is not a preposition but part of the infinitive form of the verb. An example of an infinitive used as a noun is: "To exercise is important." In this example, "to exercise" is the subject of the sentence. An example of an infinitive used as an adjective is: "She had the wisdom to travel." The infinitive "to travel" modifies "wisdom." In the sentence, "We were happy to leave," the infinitive is an adverb that modifies the adjective "happy."

Moods of verbs

There are five moods that verbs can be formed in. The *indicative* is where a statement is made: "He leaves the house at 8 am." In the *interrogative*, a question is asked: "When does he leave the house?" The *imperative* is used for commands: "Leave the house at once!" In the *conditional*, a condition or wish is stated: "If he were smart, he would leave the house earlier." And in the *subjective*, a demand, recommendation, suggestion, or statement of necessity is made: "It is necessary that he be here on time." In the subjective and conditional forms, the verbs are distinctly different. For instance, in the example "If he were smart, he would leave the house earlier," the verb is a plural form rather than a singular form. In the sentence, "It is necessary that he be here on time" the correct verb form is "be" rather than "is."

Decide what error the following sentence has and how to correct it.

> To patch an inner tube, it is necessary that the cyclist is prepared.

This sentence is incorrect grammatically because the verb form is not the right one. The sentence is a recommendation and therefore requires a subjective verb form. The verb forms "am, "is" and "are" are replaced in a subjective sentence with the verb form "be." The corrected sentence would read: "To patch an inner tube, it is necessary that the cyclist be prepared." The choice of an incorrect verb form is very common. Subjective verb forms are used in formal language but not as much in colloquial English. The subjective voice is used for a sentence that indirectly expresses a demand, recommendation, suggestion or statement of necessity.

Read the following sentence and correct it.

> When the doctor turned on the instrument, a strange sound was heard.

This sentence is an example of an incorrect shift in the voice of the verb, something that is very common in colloquial English. The sentence starts out with an active verb, "turned on," and then shifts to a passive voice with "was heard." It can be corrected by rewording the second part of the sentence; the correct sentence reads: "When the doctor turned on the instrument, he heard a strange sound." Now both verb forms are in the active voice. The pronoun "he" agrees with its precedent "doctor." The active voice is preferred because it is stronger and more direct than the passive voice.

Read the following sentence and explain why and how it needs to be corrected.

Take a dose of medicine and then you should get some sleep.

This sentence shifts from an imperative verb mood to an indicative one. The verb moods in a sentence should match and these do not. There are two ways the sentence could be changed so the verb moods agree. Both verbs could be changed so they are in the imperative form. After doing this, the sentence would read: "Take a dose of medicine and get some sleep." You could also change both verbs to the indicative mood form: "You should take a dose of medicine and then you should get some sleep." Either sentence would be correct, although the second form is overly wordy. A shorter way of saying it would be: "You should take a dose of medicine and then get some sleep," where the second "you should" is understood.

Uses for the following punctuation marks: comma, ellipsis, and dash

Sometimes a comma, an ellipsis, and a dash are used to show that there should be a pause when text is read or spoken. A comma most often shows the need for a pause for before-and-after adverbs such as "therefore," "as a result," "however," "consequently" or before adverbs like "but," "while," and "so." A comma can be used after an introductory clause to show a pause as well. An ellipsis, or three small dots, can be used to show a pause in speaking when it is in the middle of a sentence that joins two ideas. A dash can also be used to show a pause when a parenthetical phrase is inserted into a sentence. However, the comma, ellipsis and dash are also used for other reasons, so do not assume that these are their only uses.

Correct the following sentence.

The news was however not as good as it might have been about the faltering ship.

There should be a comma before and after the word "however" to show that there is a pause. When reading a sentence like this, the voice naturally wants to pause around the word "however," which is the reason commas are placed around it. "However" is a conjunction and commas often set off conjunctions to allow for a pause. There are other reasons that commas are used as well. They are used to separate items on a list, for example. They are also used in the introduction and conclusion of a letter. The corrected sentence should read: "The news was, however, not as good as it might have been about the faltering ship."

Ellipsis

An ellipsis is used to show that a portion of a quote has been omitted. An ellipsis, which consists of three small dots, can come at the beginning, middle, or end of a quotation. The ellipsis should follow any existent punctuation in the quote. For example, the entire text of this quotation from John Donne is as follows: "No man is an island, entire of itself; every man is a piece of the continent, a part of the main." If you wished to omit a portion of the text, for instance the words "entire of itself," then you would punctuate it as, "No man is an

- 76 -

island, … every man is a piece of the continent, a part of the main." When omitting something that comes after a period, put the period first and then three dots.

Correct the spelling errors in the following sentence.

He put his foot on the accelerater and drove very quickely to the grandeose palace that the movie was using for it's setting.

The words that are misspelled are: "accelerater," which is spelled "accelerator"; "quickely," which is spelled "quickly"; "grandeose," which is spelled "grandiose"; and "it's," which should be "its." When writing, make sure to check in a dictionary to see how a word is spelled if you are unsure. Certain spelling rules will help, such as "I before E, except after C," (as in the word "receive") as well as "drop the final E" ("make" becomes "making,") and "double the last consonant" ("chop" becomes "chopping"). There are other skills that you can use to help you spell words correctly, such as sounding out words. By breaking longer words down into syllables, affixes and roots you may be able to determine the way a word is spelled. And in today's world, poor spellers are also assisted by software in word processing programs, such as spell check, which automatically lets you know if it suspects that a word is misspelled, although it is not 100 percent accurate.

Read the following sentence and change the verb to an active voice.

The team was praised by the coach because of its record of wins.

To change the verb to an active voice the sentence should be rewritten as the following:

The coach praised the team because of its record of wins.

The active voice is usually preferred because it is stronger. The passive voice can be used for effect, or might be used because no one knows who or what had caused an action. For instance, in the sentence, "The ball was broken," the reason the verb must be in the passive voice is that the reason the ball was broken is unknown. The passive voice is used when the writer does not want to emphasize the doer. It is frequently used in scientific texts.

Read the following sentence and analyze the verb.

They spoke to her as if she were a child.
The verb form in the phrase "as if she were a child" is in the conditional form because it states a condition or a wish that is contrary to fact. Notice that this use of the conditional always requires the past tense. It also requires the plural form of the verb rather than the singular form. English speakers often make a mistake with the choice of verb. Although the conditional and subjunctive verb forms are not used a great deal in spoken English, they should be used when writing formal English.

Using context clues

Context clues are often found in the sentence that contains a new word or phrase as well as the sentences before and after it. A reader can often determine the meaning of an unknown word from these clues. For instance, a passage might say that the media have disseminated many foolish ideas about alligators. A reader might not be familiar with the word "disseminated," but then the passage goes on to say that some movies have implied that alligators spend their days waiting to attack an unsuspecting human being but, in fact, alligators usually feed on small animals like fish, snakes, and turtles, which live in or near the water and that it is very rare for an alligator to attack a human being. If you read this passage carefully, you can deduce that "disseminated" means "spread around." In this case, it means the spreading around of misinformation about alligators. Another helpful clue is that the word "disseminated" is in the position where a verb would go, so you would need another verb to take its place.

Use context clues to determine the meaning of "attribute" in the following excerpt.

> Some of the attributes of mammals are a backbone, warm blood, and the production of milk to nurse their young. In addition, almost all mammals bear living young. The platypus and the spiny anteater are exceptions. They lay eggs instead.

To determine the meaning of the word "attribute," the reader needs to analyze the rest of the sentence as well as the following sentences. It would appear that the excerpt is telling what mammals are like and what they have in common, with two exceptions. The excerpt says that mammals have a backbone, warm blood and that they produce milk to nurse their young. The word "attribute" as it is used is a noun, so you would look for another noun to replace it. If you substitute the words "trait" or "characteristic" for "attribute," the sentence seems to make sense. This is the way you can determine what a word or phrase means from the context clues that surround it.

Affixes and root words

A *root word* is a word before it is added onto. An *affix* is a prefix or suffix that is added onto a root word. Often, the affixes in the English language come from Latin or Greek origins. A *prefix* is added to the front of a root word and a *suffix* is added to the end of a root word. When you look at the meaning of a root word and the meaning of any affixes added to the root word, you can determine the approximate meaning of the word. For example, the root word "satisfied" means to be content with something. The prefix *dis-* means not. The reader can therefore determine that "dissatisfied" means to be not content with something.

Determine how the root and affixes of the word "precede" can help you determine its meaning.

You can determine the meaning of a word by studying its root and affixes. In the word "precede," the prefix *pre-* means "before." The root word "cede" comes from the Latin word "cedere," which means "to go." So the meaning of "precede" is fairly straightforward: it means "to go before." It is important for students to understand and study lists of prefixes and suffixes as well as root words and their meanings. This is a particularly good way to increase vocabulary and understand the origins of words. It is also useful when there is no context on which to determine the meaning of an unknown word.

Use general and specialized reference materials to find the pronunciation of a word

A print or digital dictionary can be used as a means to learn many things about a word. It will show the correct pronunciation of a word, tell its meaning, and its part of speech. The dictionary has a guide that shows how to sound out the words. It also lists all of the parts of speech that a word can be used as and the meanings it has in each form. In addition to the dictionary, the thesaurus is an extremely useful tool because it lists synonyms for all the various meanings a word can have, which helps you clarify the precise meaning as used in the context of the text you are reading. This means you can find other words to use in a report or text that mean the same as a word that may be used too often. Many books will have a glossary to help you with difficult or even technical words used in the text.

Anita was trying to verify the meaning of "brush" in the following sentence.

> She used her dictionary and found this.
> brush (brŭsh) *n.* 1. A device with bristles. 2. A light touch in passing. 3. Contact with something dangerous. *v. tr.* 4. To clean with a broom. 5. To touch lightly in passing.
Choose the correct definition of "brush" from the following sentence.

> Peter brushed by me to get to the buffet.

The correct answer is meaning 5: "to touch lightly in passing." If you substitute that definition for the word, the sentence makes sense. Meanings 1, 2, and 3 are nouns and do not fit with the context of the sentence. Meanings 4 and 5 are verbs and "brush" is used here as a verb, so it would have to be one of these definitions. When considering which meaning is being used, always check for context clues in the sentence or in the sentences before or after the sentence in which the word is used. Dictionaries also tell you how to pronounce words and what part of speech they are.

Verbal irony and puns

Verbal irony is a figure of speech in which the intended meaning of a statement actually is different, and usually the opposite, of what is said. It is often sarcastic in nature, as in the retort of the mother whose child is playing with her food and says, "Do I have to eat this food?" The mother simply says, "No, of course you don't have to eat it. Just eat it tomorrow when you are really hungry." The mother does not mean what she says in reality, but she makes the point that the food will still be there for tomorrow. A *pun* is a play on words: "He said that he would like to axe me a question, but he didn't think it would be knife to butt in on me."

Relationships between words

The relationships between words can often enlighten a reader as to their meaning. For instance, you may come across the word "colossal" and not understand what it means, but then you are told that it means the opposite of "little," giving you a good clue to its meaning. The same is true of synonyms. If someone said a synonym for "minuscule" is "tiny," you would understand the meaning of the word at once. Analogies can also be useful for understanding the meaning of words. If you are told that "foot" is to "toe" as "paw" is to "pad," then you get an idea of what a pad is from the analogy.

Distinguishing between the connotations and denotations of words

The *denotation* of a word is the dictionary definition of the word. The *connotation* of a word is what the word suggests beyond its dictionary meaning. It is both the meaning that people associate with that word and a subjective interpretation of the meaning of the word. The denotation meaning is objective. For instance, the words "bullheaded" and "resolute" mean "firm" or "persistent." But "bullheaded" carries a negative connotation because it suggests someone who is very stubborn. "Resolute," on the other hand, has better connotations because there is no suggestion that the term means "unreasonable." When you read, you should pay attention to the language that a writer uses to describe something. Look for words that suggest something about a place or person that are not directly stated in the text.

Determine what the connotations are of the words "audacious" and "brash"

The connotations of "audacious" and "brash" are different. While they both technically mean "bold," the word "brash" has a more negative connotation because it suggests someone who is hasty or even foolhardy. It could also suggest someone who is somewhat impolite. On the other hand, "audacious" has a slightly positive connotation because it means "daring" or "taking a chance" in a good way, possibly being brave. Writers often give their readers clues about characters, events, or places through the use of words that have strong connotations. It is important to study language used to describe things and people so such clues are not lost on the reader.

Improving comprehension

The acquisition of general academic and domain-specific words and phrases is especially important for success in academic endeavors. Without the ability to understand language at the high school level, a student will not be prepared for what he or she will encounter in the future, neither academically nor in life. Students must be familiar with domain-specific words and phrases if they hope to excel in a specific field. One excellent way to become proficient in language is to make lists of new words, use them in sentences, and learn to spell them. The glossary of a textbook is a good source for finding domain-specific words. Extended reading will allow the student to improve his or her vocabulary. Again, a good reader will try to understand the meaning of a word through context; should that fail, a student should find the precise meaning in a dictionary or glossary.

Mathematics Practice Test #1

Practice Questions

1. If $\frac{5}{8}$ is converted into a decimal, how many decimal places will it contain?

    Ⓐ 2

    ● 3

    Ⓒ 5

    Ⓓ 4

2. Draw a dot on the number line that corresponds to $\sqrt{7}$?.

3. If a cube has a volume of 27 cubic inches, what is the length of one edge of the cube?

    Ⓐ $x = -9$

    Ⓑ $x = 9$

    Ⓒ $x = -3$

    ● $x = 3$

$27 = l \cdot w \cdot H$ — cube so all =

$27 = x^3$

$27 = 3 \cdot 3 \cdot 3$

9 / 27

$27 = 3^3$

4. Use the grid below to draw a graph that represents the equation $y = 4x$?

5. Jonas walks at half the pace of his jogging speed. Draw a graph that shows how far he has gone after x minutes.

- 82 -

6. Given the following line, write an equation in slope intercept form.

_____

7. Graph the function that is represented by the table below.

x	y
-2	-1
0	3
1	5
3	9

8. Which of the following equations have infinitely many solutions?

Ⓐ $3(2x - 5) = 6x - 15$

Ⓑ $4x - 8 = 12$

Ⓒ $5 = 10x - 15$

Ⓓ $7x = 2x + 35$

9. Solve the equation for x: $3(x - 1) = 2(3x - 9)$

Ⓐ $x = 2$

Ⓑ $x = \frac{8}{3}$

Ⓒ $x = -5$

Ⓓ $x = 5$

10. John was given the folowing equation and asked to solve for x. $\frac{2}{3}x - 1 = 5$. His solution is shown below. Circle the step where he made a mistake and then choose the answer choice that fixes it.

$$\frac{2}{3}x - 1 = 5$$

$$\frac{2}{3}x = 4$$

$$x = \frac{4}{\left(\frac{2}{3}\right)}$$

$$x = 6$$

Ⓐ $\frac{2}{3}x = 8$

Ⓑ $\frac{2}{3}x = 6$

Ⓒ $x = 8$

Ⓓ $x = \frac{2}{\left(\frac{2}{3}\right)}$

11. Graph a system of two linear equations that has a single solution at (1, 4).

12. Which point represents the solution to the system of linear equations graphed below?

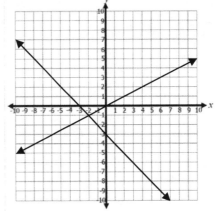

   Ⓐ $(0, 0)$

   Ⓑ $(0, -3)$

   Ⓒ $(-2, -1)$

   Ⓓ $(-3, 0)$

13. Solve the system of linear equations. $\begin{cases} 3x - 2y = -10 \\ y = 2x + 5 \end{cases}$

   Ⓐ $(0, 5)$

   Ⓑ $(-2, 1)$

   Ⓒ $(1, 2)$

   Ⓓ $(-3, -4)$

14. **Solve the system of linear equations.** $\begin{cases} 5x - y = -41 \\ 3x + y = -15 \end{cases}$

    Ⓐ $(1, -18)$

    Ⓑ $(-6, 3)$

    Ⓒ $(-8, 1)$

    Ⓓ $(-7, 6)$

15. **The sum of two numbers is 12. Kelly says the difference of these two numbers must be more than 3. Give an example that supports her claim, and an example that shows her claim is false.**

Supports Kelly's claim

☐ – ☐ = ☐

Shows Kelly's claim is false

☐ – ☐ = ☐

16. **The sum of two numbers is 6. The second number is three more than twice the first number. What are the two numbers?**

    Ⓐ 0 and 6

    Ⓑ 3 and 3

    Ⓒ 2 and 4

    Ⓓ 1 and 5

17. **What is the y-intercept of the line $y = 4x - 6$?**

    Ⓐ -4

    Ⓑ 4

    Ⓒ 6

    Ⓓ -6

18. Which function has the higher maximum output?

Function I

x	y
2	3
4	10
5	3

Function II

Ⓐ Function I

Ⓑ Function II

Ⓒ They have the same maximum output.

Ⓓ Cannot be determined

19. Which function has the greater rate of change?

Function I

x	y
2	4
3	6
4	8

Function II

$y = 5x - 1$

Ⓐ Function I

Ⓑ Function II

Ⓒ They have the same rate of change.

Ⓓ Cannot be determined

20. Using the triangle below, which equation would be used to solve for the missing side?

Ⓐ $x = \sqrt{16^2 + 30^2}$

Ⓑ $x = \sqrt{30^2 - 16^2}$

Ⓒ $16 = \sqrt{30^2 - x^2}$

Ⓓ $16 = \sqrt{30^2 + x^2}$

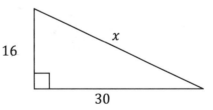

21. Which linear function represents the values in the table?

x	0	1	2	3
y	3	1	−1	−3

Ⓐ $y = -2x + 1$

Ⓑ $y = 2x + 3$

Ⓒ $y = 3x + 1$

Ⓓ $y = -2x + 3$

- 87 -

22. Look at the graph below. Which equation represents a function with a greater slope?

Ⓐ $y = x - 2$

Ⓑ $y = 2x - 2$

Ⓒ $y = \frac{1}{2}x - 1$

Ⓓ $y = x - 4$

23. Which graph best represents the situation?

You leave your house and go to school, you spend the day there, then return home.

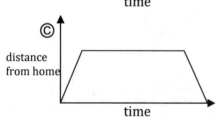

24. Which preimage and image represent a reflection?

25. Given the image below, what transformation did it undergo?

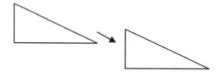

Ⓐ Translation

Ⓑ Dilation

Ⓒ Reflection

Ⓓ Rotation

Use the figure to the right to answer questions 26 and 27:
26. If △ABC translated 4 units left, what ordered pair would point A map onto?

27. If △ABC is reflected across the x-axis what ordered pair would point C map onto?

Ⓐ (−7, 2)

Ⓑ (2, 7)

Ⓒ (7, −2)

Ⓓ (−2, 7)

28. What two transformations will map figure *A* onto figure *B*?

    Ⓐ Rotation and Translation

    Ⓑ Translation and Reflection

    Ⓒ Translation and Dilation

    Ⓓ Reflection and Rotation

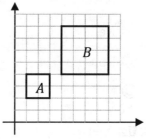

29. Two sides of a right triangle are $\sqrt{17}$ units and $\sqrt{8}$ units. There are two possible lengths for the third side.

What is the shortest possible length, in units? _____

What is the longest possible length, in units? _____

30. Given the graph below draw a rectangle with a perimeter of 30 units. The length of the side of each square is a unit.

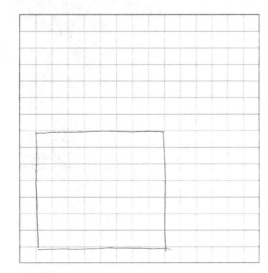

31. How many cubic feet of grain will fill the silo if the silo is completely full?

    Ⓐ 753.6 ft³

    Ⓑ 6028.8 ft³

    Ⓒ 1920 ft³

    Ⓓ 22608 *ft³*

32. What kind of association does the scatter plot show?

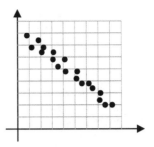

Ⓐ Positive, Linear Association

Ⓑ Negative, Linear Association

Ⓒ Non-linear Association

Ⓓ No association can be determined

33. Using the data below, what information was gathered correctly?

Favorite type of music		Age of student surveyed			
		6-8	9-11	12-14	15-17
	Pop				
	Hip Hop	12	45	50	40
	Country	10	20	45	55
	Other	8	15	20	25
	Pop	8	10	8	20

Ⓐ More students prefer country music to pop music.

Ⓑ Pop music is preferred to Hip Hop by more students in the 15-17 age category.

Ⓒ Hip Hop is preferred to country music by more students in the 9-11 age group.

Ⓓ Pop music is preferred to Hip Hop by more students in the 12-14 age group.

34. On the graph below, draw a triangle with a base of 8 units, and a height of 5 units. The length of the side of each square is one unit.

35. David surveyed 10 people to find out whether they owned a car or a truck or both. Using the information below complete the table.

50% owned a car.

30% owned a truck.

10% owned both a car and a truck.

	Car	No Car	Total
Truck			
No Truck			
Total			10

36. Bananas cost $.50 per pound. On the graph below, draw a line that shows the proportional relationship between the number of pounds and the cost.

37. A sphere and a cylinder have the same volume. Each figure has a radius of 4 inches. What is the height of the cylinder?

ⓐ $5\frac{1}{2}$

ⓑ $5\frac{1}{3}$

ⓒ $3\frac{1}{5}$

ⓓ $3\frac{1}{2}$

38. Jane is buying oranges. Store A sells oranges 4 for $7, while store B sells oranges 5 for $9. Which store has a better price? Explain you answer.

_____

_____

_____

39. Look at the figure on the graph below. Draw the new image of the figure after the following transformations.

- A reflection across the x-axis
- A horizontal translation 5 units to the left

40. Josh and Kate each wrote down a different function. The slope of their functions is the same. Josh's function is $y = 4x - 9$. Give a function that could be Kate's function.

_____

Answers and Explanations

1. B: $\frac{5}{8}$ as a decimal is .625. That is 3 decimal places.

2. The square root of 7 is approximately 2.64. The dot should be placed like so:

3. D: The volume of a cube is found by cubing the length of one edge of the cube. So given a volume and asked to find the length of the edge of a cube simply take the cube root of the volume.

$$x^3 = 27$$
$$\sqrt[3]{x^3} = \sqrt[3]{27}$$
$$x = 3$$

4. The equation is in slope-intercept form of $y = mx + b$. In the equation, the slope is 4 and the y-intercept is 0. So the first point is (0,0) because of the y-intercept, and since the slope is 4, the next point moves 4 spaces up and 1 to the right to the point (1,4).

5. If Jonas walks at half the pace he jogs then he will only cover half on the distance when walking. The line is shown below.

6. To write an equation, first find several points on the graph. For example, (0,0), (2,1), (4,2). To write an equation in slope intercept form first find the y-intercept. This is the point where x=0. Since one of the points we found is (0,0), we know the y-intercept is 0. Next, find slope of the line, which is the change in y over the change in x. For this example it would be $\frac{2-1}{4-2}$, so the slope is $\frac{1}{2}$. The equation of this line is $y = \frac{1}{2}x$.

7. To graph a line from a table, first plot all of the points on the graph, and the draw a line that connects all of the points.

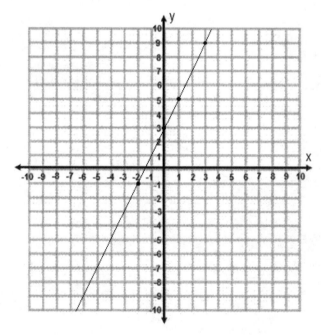

8. A: A is the only one that has infinitely many solutions because when the 3 is distributed across the parentheses, the resulting equation is $6x - 15 = 6x - 15$. Because each side of the equation is identical to the other side, any value of x will make a true statement, so there are infinitely many solutions.

9. D: $3(x - 1) = 2(3x - 9)$
$3x - 3 = 6x - 18$ Distribute
$-3 = 3x - 18$ Subtract $3x$ from both sides
$15 = 3x$ Add 18 to both sides
$5 = x$ Divide both sides by 3

10. B. The answer that John gave was:

$$\frac{2}{3}x - 1 = 5$$
$$\frac{2}{3}x = 4$$
$$x = \frac{4}{\left(\frac{2}{3}\right)}$$
$$x = 6$$

However, he messed up on the second step when he moved the -1 across it should have become a positive 1. That step should be $\frac{2}{3}x = 6$.

11. A system of linear equations is a set of linear equations that involve the same set of variables. In this case those variables are x and y. For a system of equations to have only one solution they must only meet once. In this problem the point where they intersect is $(1, 4)$. So, any two linear equations that intersect only at the point $(1, 4)$ are a solution to this problem. An example is graphed below.

12. C: Given the graph of a system of linear equations, the solution is the point of intersection of the two lines. In this graph, the two lines intersect at $(-2, -1)$.

13. A: $3x - 2(2x + 5) = -10$ Substitute the expression for y into the other equation
$3x - 4x - 10 = -10$ Distribute the -2 across the parentheses
$-x - 10 = -10$ Combine like terms
$-x = 0$ Add 10 to both sides
$x = 0$ Divide by -1
$y = 2(0) + 5 = 5$ Substitute the value of x into the original equation and simplify.

(0,5)   Write your final answer as an ordered pair (x, y)

14. D:
$\begin{aligned}5x - y &= -41 \\ 3x + y &= -15\end{aligned}$ the y terms are opposites of each other, use the elimination method.

$8x = -56$	Add the two equations together to get this equation
$x = -7$	Divide both sides by 8
$3(-7) + y = -15$	Substitute the value of x into one of the original equations
$-21 + y = -15$	Multiply
$y = 6$	Add 21 to both sides
$(-7, 6)$	Write your final answer as an ordered pair (x, y)

15. The numbers must add up to equal 12, and one set should have a difference greater than 3 and the other set should have a difference less than 3. An example is given below:

$$\boxed{8} - \boxed{4} = \boxed{4}$$

$$\boxed{7} - \boxed{5} = \boxed{2}$$

$8 + 4 = 12$, and the difference is greater than 3.
$7 + 5 = 12$, and the difference is less than 3.

16. D: All choices add up to 6, but only the number 5 is three more than twice 1.
Also, the system $\begin{aligned}x + y &= 6 \\ y &= 2x + 3\end{aligned}$ can be used to solve the system. The solution is shown below:

$x + (2x + 3) = 6$	Substitute the expression for y into the first equation
$x + 2x + 3 = 6$	Remove parentheses
$3x + 3 = 6$	Combine like terms
$3x = 3$	Subtract 3 from both sides
$x = 1$	Divide by 3 on both sides
$y = 2(1) + 3 = 5$	Substitute value into original equation and simplify

1 and 5

17. D: The line is written in slope-intercept form: $y = mx + b$, and b is the y-intercept. The number that corresponds with b is -6.

18. A: The maximum output in Function I is 10. The maximum output in Function II is 2. Ten is greater than two, so Function I has the higher maximum output.

19. B: The rate of change is also the slope of the linear function, that is, the vertical change over horizontal change. The rate of change for Function I is 2, because the y-value increases 2 for every 1 the input increases. The rate of change for Function II is 5. Function II is written in slope-intercept form and the number that corresponds to the slope is 5. Since 5 is greater than 2, Function II has the greater rate of change.

20. A: The Pythagorean Theorem, $a^2 + b^2 = c^2$, states that the sum of the squares of the legs equals the square of the hypotenuse. Therefore, the hypotenuse is equal to the square root of the sum of the squares of the legs. The legs of the triangle are 16 and 30. The hypotenuse is x. The equation solved for the value of the hypotenuse will be $x = \sqrt{16^2 + 30^2}$.

21. D: Based on the table, the rate of change is -2 and the y-intercept is $(0, 3)$. Plugging this information into the slope-intercept form $y = mx + b$, the equation is $y = -2x + 3$.

22. B: The y-intercept of the line is $(0, -1)$. Another point on the line is $(1,0)$. Slope is the vertical change over horizontal change which is $\frac{1}{1} = 1$. The answer choices are already given in slope-intercept form, so you just have to pick the one with a greater slope than 1. The only one that has a greater slope is 2x-2.

23. C: Since the graphs show the distance from home, and it start at home, the graph begins at the origin. When arriving at school and staying there, the graph is horizontal because the distance from home doesn't change. Then when returning home, the graph returns to the x-axis. Answer C is the only one that shows all three parts.

24. A: Answer A is the only one that represents a reflection or "flip". Answer B represents a translation or "slide". Answer C represents a rotation or turn. Answer D represents a dilation or changing size.

25. A: Answer A is the only one that represents a translation or "slide". Answer B represents a reflection or "flip". Answer C is a dilation. Answer D is a rotation or "turn."

26. Point A starts at the ordered pair $(7, 8)$. If it is translated four units left it would end up at the ordered pair $(3, 8)$.

27. C: Point C starts at the ordered pair $(7, 2)$. If it is reflected across the x-axis it would end up at the ordered pair $(7-2)$.

28. C: Since the size of B is different from the size of A, a dilation must occur. The only option that has a dilation is C.

29. The Pythagorean Theorem $(a^2 + b^2 = c^2)$ can be used to find the missing side of a right triangle. Given two side measurements the third side can be either the hypotenuse or one of the shorter sides. The shortest possible length for this side can be found by making $\sqrt{17}$ the hypotenuse. The equation would be $\left(\sqrt{8}\right)^2 + b^2 = \left(\sqrt{17}\right)^2$. So, $8 + b^2 = 17, b^2 = 9, b = 3$. The shortest the third side could be is 3 units. The equation for the longest possible length would be, $\left(\sqrt{8}\right)^2 + \left(\sqrt{17}\right)^2 = c^2$. So, $8 + 17 = c^2, c^2 = 25$, c=5. The longest possible length the third side can be is 5 units.

30. The perimeter of a rectangle is found by adding up the lengths of all of the sides. So, any rectangle that has side lengths that add up to 30 would work. The example below shows a 5 by 6 rectangle.

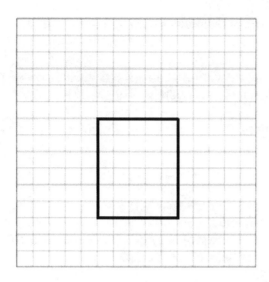

31. B: The formula for the volume of a cylinder is $V = \pi r^2 h$. All values are placed into the formula and simplified. The work is shown below:

$$V = (3.14)(8\ ft)^2(30\ ft)$$
$$V = (3.14)(64\ ft^2)(30\ ft)$$
$$V = 6028.8\ ft^3$$

32. B: A single straight line can be drawn that is close to many of the points. The slope of that line would be negative, so the points have a negative, linear association.

33. D: Answer D is correct because 50 is greater than 45, so pop music is preferred to hip hop by more students in the age group of 12-14.

34. The triangle below has a base of 8 units and a height of 5 units.

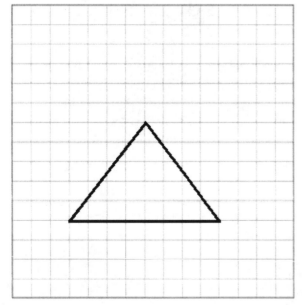

35. Start in the upper leftmost corner. Since 10% own both, that means that 1 person owns both. Then 30% own a truck, so 3 people own a truck but 1 of those owns both. So, only 2

people own just a truck. Then 50% own a car, but one of them owns both, so only 4 own just a car. That leaves 3 people that don't own either one. Add up the columns and rows to get totals and the answer looks like this:

	Car	No Car	Total
Truck	1	2	3
No Truck	4	3	7
Total	5	5	10

36. If bananas cost $.50 per pound then for every 2 pounds it would cost $1. The graph that represents this would look like:

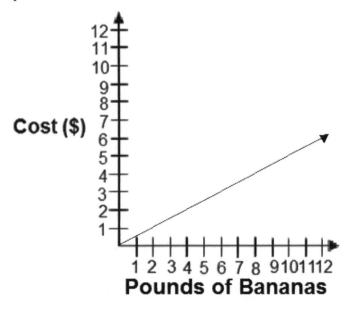

37. B: The volume of a sphere is, $V = \frac{4}{3}\pi r^3$, and the volume of a cylinder is, $V = \pi r^2 h$. Since we know the radius we can solve for the volume of the sphere and we get $V = \frac{4}{3}\pi(4)^3 = 268.08257$ cubic inches. Then, begin to solve for the volume of the cylinder $V = \pi(4)^2 h = 268.08257$. So, $50.26548h = 268.08257$, and $h = 5\frac{1}{3}$.

38. If Store A sells oranges 4 for $7, then divide 7 by 4 to figure out their cost per orange. 7/4=$1.75 per orange. Store B sells them 5 for $9, so 9/5=$1.80 per orange. This means that Store A has the better price on oranges.

- 101 -

39. A reflection is a transformation where each point on a shape appears at an equal distance on the opposite side of the line of reflection. In this case the line of reflection is the x-axis. After the reflection the image was translated left 5 units. A translation is simply just "sliding" the image. After these two transformations the image would look like this.

40. Josh's function is $4x - 9$, which means his has a slope of 4. That means Kate's function can be anything with a slope of 4. So for example, hers could be $4x + 2$.

Mathematics Practice Test #2

Practice Test

1. Which fraction is equivalent to 0.375?

(A) $\frac{4}{25}$

(B) $\frac{1}{6}$

(C) $\frac{3}{8}$

(D) $\frac{3}{20}$

2. $2\sqrt{5}$ is between which two numbers?

(A) 4 and 5

(B) 2 and 3

(C) 3 and 4

(D) 10 and 11

3. A square has an area of 64 square units. What is the length of one side square?

(A) 7

(B) 6

(C) 10

(D) 8

4. The total length of the world's coastlines is about 315,000 miles. Which answer expresses this in scientific notation?

(A) 3.15×10^{-6}

(B) 3.15×10^{-5}

(C) 3.15×10^{6}

(D) 3.15×10^{5}

5. Marla is a growing a plant. The plants growth is graphed below. Based on the graph how many feet does the plant grow each week?

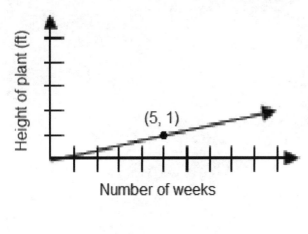

_____feet

6. John's Gym charges its members according to the equation $C = 40m$ where m is the number of months and C represents the total cost to each customer after m months. Ralph's Recreation Room charges its members according to the equation $C = 45m$. What relationship can be determined about the monthly cost to the members of each company?

Ⓐ John's monthly membership fee is equal to Ralph's monthly membership fee.

Ⓑ John's monthly membership fee is more than Ralph's monthly membership fee.

Ⓒ John's monthly membership fee is less than Ralph's monthly membership fee.

Ⓓ No relationship between the monthly membership fees can be determined.

7. What relationship can be determined about the slopes of line p and line q?

Ⓐ The slope of line p is equal to the slope of line q.

Ⓑ The slope of line p is greater than the slope of line q.

Ⓒ The slope of line p is less than the slope of line q.

Ⓓ No relationship can be determined from the graph.

SSSSSSSSSSSSSSSSSSSSSSSSSSSSSSSSSSSSSSSSSSSSSSSSSSSSSSSSSSSSSSSSSSSSSSSSSSSSSꙄꙄꙄꙄꙄꙄꙄꙄꙄꙄꙄꙄꙄꙄꙄꙄꙄꙄꙄꙄ
SSSSSSSSSSSSSSSSSSSSSSSSSSSSSSSSSSSSSSSSSSSSSSSSSSSSSSSSSSSSSSSSSSSSSSSSSSSSSSSSS

8. Write an equation for line m in slope-intercept form.

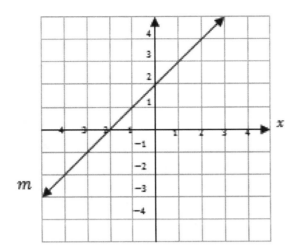

_____

9. Given the equation $+1 = \_x + \_$. Create an equation with no solutions, one solution, and infinitely many solutions.

Equation with no solutions

$$6x + 1 = \boxed{}x + \boxed{}$$

Equation with one solution

$$6x + 1 = \boxed{3}x + \boxed{2}$$

Equation with infinitely many solutions

$$6x + 1 = \boxed{}x + \boxed{}$$

10. How many solutions does the equation $2(7x - 5) = 14x - 8$ have?

Ⓐ None

Ⓑ One

Ⓒ Two

Ⓓ Infinitely many solutions

11. Solve the equation for x. $\frac{1}{2}(x-7) = \frac{3}{5}(5x+15)$

Ⓐ $x = -\frac{16}{5}$

Ⓑ $x = \frac{16}{5}$

Ⓒ $x = 5$

Ⓓ $x = -5$

12. Which point is a solution to the system $\begin{cases} 2x+y=7 \\ x-y=2 \end{cases}$?

Ⓐ $(4,-1)$

Ⓑ $(2,3)$

Ⓒ $(3,1)$

Ⓓ $(5,3)$

13. Solve the system of linear equations $\begin{cases} y=-x+3 \\ y=\frac{1}{2}x+9 \end{cases}$.

Ⓐ $(1,2)$

Ⓑ $(-4,7)$

Ⓒ $(4,-1)$

Ⓓ $(6,12)$

14. Mark and Sally were selling candy bars for their school fundraiser. Together they sold 49 candy bars. Sally sold one less than four times the amount Mark sold. How many candy bars did Sally sell?

Ⓐ 29

Ⓑ 34

Ⓒ 39

Ⓓ 44

15. A school auditorium has 600 seats total on the main floor and balcony combined. There are 5 times as many seats on the main floor than there are in the balcony. Based on this information fill in the equation below.

Seats on   **+**   Seats in   **=**   Total number
main floor   balcony   of seats

16. Which of the following graphs is <u>not</u> a function?

Ⓐ

Ⓑ

Ⓒ

Ⓓ

17. Which transformations can be done to image *A* to produce image *B*? Circle all that apply.

Translation

Rotation

Reflection

A   *B*

Dilation

18. Which function has the smaller range?

 Ⓐ Function I

 Ⓑ Functions II

 Ⓒ They have the same y-intercept

 Ⓓ Cannot be determined

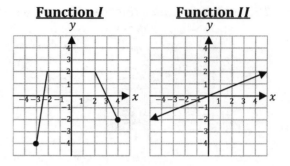

Function *I*   Function *II*

19. Which function below is <u>not</u> linear?

 Ⓐ $4y + 3x = -1$

 Ⓑ $2x - y = 5$

 Ⓒ $y = 3x - 9$ ✓

 Ⓓ $y = \sqrt{x} + 2$

20. Write a function in slope-intercept form based on the values in the table?

x	0	2	4	5
y	-2	8	18	23

_____

21. Which function represents the graph?

 Ⓐ $y = 3x + 1$

 Ⓑ $y = 3x - 3$

 Ⓒ $y = -3x + 1$

 Ⓓ $y = -3x - 3$

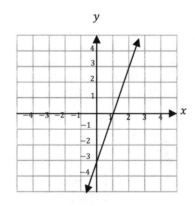

- 108 -

22. On which interval is the function decreasing?

___ < **x** < ___

23. Which graph best represents the situation?
The speed of your bike as you start rolling down a hill without pedaling, pedal at a constant rate on a level sidewalk, and stop at a store.

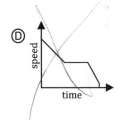

24. Which two shapes represent a rotation?

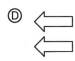

25. What transformation do the two shapes below represent?

_____

26. If △ABC is dilated by a factor of 3, what is the new measure of $\overline{AB}$?

Ⓐ 2

Ⓑ 6

Ⓒ 9

Ⓓ 18

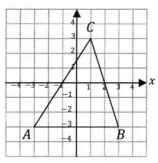

27. What two transformations will map figure A onto figure B?

Ⓐ Rotation and Translation

Ⓑ Reflection and Translation

Ⓒ Rotation and Dilation

Ⓓ Translation and Dilation

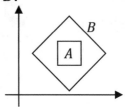

28. Given triangle △ABC, with the $m\angle C$ is 60°, and the $m\angle B$ is $\frac{2}{3}$ of $m\angle C$. What is the $m\angle A$?

Ⓐ 45°

Ⓑ 105°

Ⓒ 60°

Ⓓ 80°

29. How much more is $AB + BC$ than AC?

Ⓐ 8 cm

Ⓑ 9 cm

Ⓒ 10 cm

Ⓓ 11 cm

30. Given the two points on the graph below, what is the distance between them?

_____

31. Label the side lengths of the rectangular prism so that the volume equals 48 cu. in.

32. What is the volume of the sphere?

Ⓐ 904.32 cubic yard

Ⓑ 7234.56 cubic yards

Ⓒ 602.88 cubic yards

Ⓓ 57876.48 cubic yards

33. Which line best represents the line-of-fit for the data?

Ⓐ $y = -7x + 1$

Ⓑ $y = 7x - 1$

Ⓒ $y = -x + 7$

Ⓓ $y = x - 7$

34. Using the data at the right, what statement best describes the rate of change?

Ⓐ Every day, the snow melts 10 centimeters.

Ⓑ Every day, the snow melts 5 centimeters.

Ⓒ Every day, the snow increases by 10 centimeters.

Ⓓ Every day, the snow increases by 5 centimeters.

The number of days from now

35. Using the data below, decide if the following statement is true or false.

	Blue Eyes	Not Blue Eyes	Total
Male	15	80	95
Female	20	60	80
Total	35	140	175

A larger percentage of women have blue eyes than the percentage of men who have blue eyes.

_____

36. Blake is 3 years younger than Susie. Susie is 4 years younger than twice the age of Brett. Brett is 2 years older than Jaime and Jaime is 9 years old. Place their names on the number line below with an arrow pointing to their age.

37. A game uses a coin and two dice. To win the game a player must have both of the following results:
- The coin must land on heads when it is flipped
- The total of the dice roll must be ten or greater

What are the odds of a player winning this game?

Ⓐ $\frac{3}{8}$

Ⓑ $\frac{1}{10}$

Ⓒ $\frac{1}{8}$

Ⓓ $\frac{2}{5}$

38. Jim was given the following problem to solve. His answer and work are shown below. Circle the part of his work where he made the mistake and then rewrite that step to correct it.

A hardware store sells hammers and saws. The hammers normally cost $25, and the saws are normally $20. This week the hammers are on sale for $5 off, and the saws are on sale for 15% off. If they sell 12 hammers and 14 saws, how many dollars worth of merchandise did they sell?

$25 - \$5 = \$20, \ 20 * 12 = \$240$

$20 * .15 = \$3, \ \$3 * 14 = \$42$

$240 + \$42 = \$282$

_____

39. If triangle *ABC* undergoes the following transformations to become triangle *DEF*:
- Rotation
- Dilation
- Reflection

Is triangle *DEF* congruent to triangle *ABC*?

_____

Is triangle *DEF* similar to triangle *ABC*?

_____

40. At a donut shop, donuts cost $2 per half dozen donuts. Draw a line on the graph below that represents this relationship.

- 114 -

Answers and Explanations

1. C: Changing 0.375 into a fraction by writing $\frac{375}{1000}$ because 0.375 is in the thousandths. Then reduce the fraction by dividing the numerator and the denominator by the greatest common factor of 125 to get $\frac{3}{8}$.

2. A: Compare the square of $2\sqrt{5}$ to the square of the whole numbers. $(2\sqrt{5})^2 = 2^2\sqrt{5}^2 = 4 \times 5 = 20$. See that 20 is between 16 and 25, or 4^2 and 5^2, so $2\sqrt{5}$ is between 4 and 5. Checking with a calculator, $2\sqrt{5} \approx 4.472$

3. D: The formula for the area of a square is $A = s^2$, where s is the length of one side of the square. In this case, $64 = s^2$. To solve for s, just square root both sides of the equation and s=8.

4. D: To write a number in scientific notation, the form is $a \times 10^n$, where $1 \le a < 10$. The decimal need to move 5 spaces to the left so it is immediately to the right of the 3. Because it moved 5 spaces to the left, $n = 5$, so the answer is 3.15×10^5

5. The point on the graph is at (5,1), which shows that after 5 weeks the plant has grown 1 foot. This means that the plant grows $\frac{1}{5}$ ft. per week.

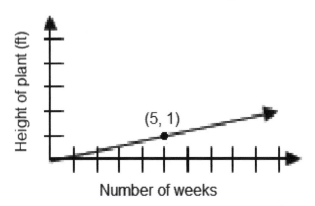

Math.Content.8.EE.5

6. C: In both equations, the coefficient of m is the rate of change. In this problem, the rate of change represents the customer's monthly cost. Therefore the customers at John's Gym pay $40 per month, and the customers at Ralph's Recreation Room pay $45 per month. Thus, John's monthly membership fee is less than Ralph's monthly membership fee.

7. A: The slope of a line is its rate of change, or vertical change over horizontal change. For every 2 the line p moves right, it moves up 1. The slope for line p is $\frac{1}{2}$ and the slope of line q is also $\frac{1}{2}$. Therefore, the slope of line p is equal to the slope of line q.

8. Writing the equation of the line in slope-intercept form $y = mx + b$, the y-intercept, b, is (0,2) and the slope, m, or rate of change is $\frac{1}{1} = 1$. Substituting these numbers into the equation the answer is $y = x + 2$.

- 115 -

9. An example of an equation with no solutions is $6x + 1 = 6x + 3$.
To solve this equation, we can subtract 6x off of both sides. This leaves 3=1 which is not true so there is no solution to this equation.

An example of an equation with one solution is $6x + 1 = 4x + 9$.
The equation is solved below:

$6x + 1 = 4x + 9$	Subtract $4x$ from both sides of the equation
$2x + 1 = 9$	Subtract 1 from both sides of the equation
$2x = 8$	Divide by 2 on both sides of the equation
$x = 4$	So there is one solution to this equation.

An example of an equation with infinite solutions is $6x + 1 = 6x + 1$. For any value of x that is plugged in each side will always equal the other side.

10. A: The equation is solved below:

$2(7x - 5) = 14x - 8$	Distribute 2 across the parentheses
$14x - 10 = 14x - 8$	Subtract $14x$ from both sides of the equation
$-10 = -8$	

Because $-10 \neq -8$, no solution exists for the equation.

11. D: The equation is solved below:

$\frac{1}{2}(x - 7) = \frac{3}{5}(5x + 15)$	
$x - 7 = \frac{6}{5}(5x + 15)$	Clear the fraction $\frac{1}{2}$ on the left by multiplying both sides by 2
$x - 7 = 6x + 18$	Distribute $\frac{6}{5}$ across the parentheses
$-7 = 5x + 18$	Subtract x from both sides
$-25 = 5x$	Subtract 18 from both sides
$-5 = x$	Divide both sides by 5

12 . C: The problem is solved below

$$\begin{cases} 2x + y = 7 \\ x - y = 2 \end{cases}$$

$3x = 9$	Because the two equations had opposite terms, add them vertically
$x = 3$	Divide both sides by 3
$2(3) + y = 7$	Substitute 3 into one of the original equations
$6 + y = 7$	Multiply
$y = 1$	Subtract 6 from both sides
$(3,1)$	Write the final answer as an ordered pair (x, y)

13. B: The answer is solved below:

$$\begin{cases} y = -x + 3 \\ y = \frac{1}{2}x + 9 \end{cases}$$

$-x + 3 = \frac{1}{2}x + 9$	Since both expressions are equal to y, set the expressions equal to each other
$3 = \frac{3}{2}x + 9$	Add x to both sides of the equation
$-6 = \frac{3}{2}x$	Subtract 9 from both sides of the equation

$-4 = x$ Multiply both sides by $\frac{2}{3}$

$y = -(-4) + 3 = 7$ Substitute the value for x into one of the original equations

$(-4, 7)$ Write the final answer as an ordered pair (x, y)

14. C: The system of linear equation that can be written from the problem is $\begin{cases} M + S = 49 \\ S = 4M - 1 \end{cases}$.

The solution to the system is below:

$M + (4M - 1) = 49$ Substitute the value for S into the other equation

$M + 4M - 1 = 49$ Remove parentheses

$5M - 1 = 49$ Combine like terms

$5M = 50$ Add 1 to both sides of the equation

$M = 10$ Divide 5 on both sides of the equation

$S = 4(10) - 1 = 39$ Substitute value of M into other equation and evaluate

Sally sold 39 candy bars.

15. The system of linear equations that can be formed from the problem is $\begin{cases} m + b = 600 \\ m = 5b \end{cases}$.

The solution to the system is below:

$(5b) + b = 600$ Substitute the expression for m into the other equation

$5b + b = 600$ Remove parentheses

$6b = 600$ Combine like terms

$b = 100$ Divide by 6 on both sides

$m = 5(100) = 500$ Substitute the value for b into the expression for m and evaluate.

So, the final equation would be $500 + 100 = 600$

16. D: A function cannot map a single input to more than one output. The vertical line test states that if a vertical line touches a graph in more than one point, then it is not a function. The graph from answer D does not pass the vertical line test so it is not a function.

17. Image A could be translated, rotated, or reflected to form image B. It cannot be dilated to form image B. A translation is just "sliding" an image to a new location. A reflection makes a mirror image on the other side of a line of reflection. A rotation just turns the image. It cannot be dialted because that would change the size of the image.

18. A: The range of the function is the set of all outputs, or y-values. The range of Function I is from-4 to 2, and the range of Function II is the set of all real numbers. Therefore the range of Function I is smaller than the range of Function II.

19. D: A function is linear if the powers of the x and y variables are 1. In answer D, the $\sqrt{x}$ $=x^{1/2}$, so its exponent is not 1, thus answer D is not linear.

20. First find the y-intercept, which is where $x = 0$. In this case it is -2. Next, find the slope of the line. Slope is equal to rise over run, or in this case $\frac{10}{2} = 5$. So, the equation in slope intercept form is y=5x-2.

21. B: The equations are in slope-intercept form. The y-intercept, b, is the point where the graph touches the y-axis. The y-intercept of this graph is $(0, -3)$. The slope, m, is the vertical change over the horizontal change. The vertical change is 3 and the horizontal change is 1

so the slope is $\frac{3}{1} = 3$. Substituting these numbers into the slope-intercept form you will get $y = 3x - 3$. /Book Error

22. On a graph, a function is increasing if the line is sloping up as it is moving from left to right. The only interval on the graph with positive slope is $2 < x < 3$.

23. A: As the bike rolls down the hill, the speed gradually increases. When the pedaling then moves to a constant rate, the speed will reach a constant rate shown by a horizontal line. When the bike stops at a store, the speed then drops to the x-axis. The only graph that shows all three parts is answer A.

24. A: A rotation, or turn, is only seen in answer A. Answer B shows a translation, or slide; answer C shows a dilation; and answer C shows a reflection or translation.

25. They represent a dilation. The shapes are congruent, one is just bigger than the other.

26. D: If a dilation has a scale factor if 3, then the length of each side is multiplied by 3 to get the new length. The measure of $\overline{AB}$ is 6, so when it is multiplied by 3 it becomes 18.

27. C: Because the two figures are different sizes, one of the transformations is a dilation. Also, the figures are turned which is a rotation. Answer C gives those two answers.

28. D: The Triangle Sum Theorem says the three angles of a triangle must add up to **180°**.
So $60° + 40° + m\angle A = 180°$
$100° + m\angle A = 180°$ Combine like terms
$m\angle A = 80°$ Subtract 105 from both sides

29. A: First solve for BC. By use of the Pythagorean Theorem $a^2 + b^2 = c^2$ and substituting the appropriate values, the equation becomes
$BC^2 + 40^2 = 41^2$
$BC^2 + 1600 = 1681$ Evaluate the exponents
$BC^2 = 81$ Subtract 1600 from both sides
$BC = 9$ Take the square root of both sides
To find how much more $AB + BC$ is compared to AC evaluate the expression $(AB + BC) - AC$. This yields $(40 + 9) - 41 = 8$.

30. The distance formula is $d = \sqrt{(x_2 - x_1)^2 + (y_2 - y_1)^2}$, and plugging in values then evaluating will get the final answer.

$$\sqrt{\left(-6 - (-3)\right)^2 + (9 - 1)^2}$$
$$\sqrt{(-3)^2 + 8^2}$$
$$\sqrt{9 + 64}$$
$$\sqrt{73} \approx 8.54$$

31. A: The volume formula for a rectangular solid is $V = lwh$. In this problem the volume is 48 cu. inches. So, and three numbers that multiply to be 48 would work. An example is given below.

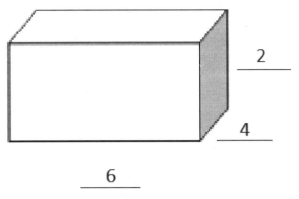

$$2 * 4 * 6 = 48$$

32. B: The volume formula for a sphere is $V = \frac{4}{3}\pi r^3$. Plugging in the value of the radius then evaluating will yield the final answer:

$$V = \frac{4}{3}(3.14)(12\ yd)^3$$
$$V = 7234.56\ yd^3$$

33. C: If a line is drawn as close to the points as possible, the y-intercept would be 7 and the slope would be -1. From this information, the line is $y = -x + 7$

34. B: If a line-of-fit is drawn through the points, the slope will be $-\frac{1}{5}$ so the snow melts 5 centimeters every day.

35. The percentage of women with blue eyes is $\frac{20}{80} = 25\%$, and the percentage of men with blue eyes is $\frac{15}{95} \approx 15.8\%$. Therefore a larger percentage of women surveyed have blue eyes then the percentage men who were surveyed that have blue eyes, and the statement is true.

36. We know that Jaime is 9, and Brett is 2 years older, so he must be 11. Susie is 4 years younger than twice Brett, so she is 18. Then Blake is 3 years younger, so he is 15. The number line should look like this.

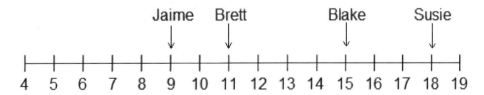

37. C: The probability of a coin landing on heads is $\frac{1}{2}$. The probability of two dice landing on 10 or better is $\frac{3}{12}$. To find the probaility of both multiply them together. So, $\frac{1}{2} * \frac{3}{12} = \frac{3}{24} = \frac{1}{8}$.

38. The place where he made a mistake was when he applied the 15% discount to the saws. He wrote $\$20 * .15 = \$3$, but they are 15% off not 15% of the original cost. So, it should be $\$20 * .85 = \$3$.

39. For two shapes to be congruent they must be the same size and same shape. If the triangle undergoes a dilation it is no longer congruent. So, triangle *DEF* is not congruen to triangle *ABC*. For two shapes to be similar they just have to be the same shape but the size can be different. In, this case triangle *DEF* is similar to triangle *ABC*.

40. If donuts are $2 per half dozen, then they are $4 per dozen. The graph below represents this relationship.

English Language Arts Practice Test #1

Practice Questions

Read the following passage from Robert Frost's poem "The Road Not Taken" to answer questions 1-5:

       Two roads diverged in a yellow wood,
       And sorry I could not travel both
       And be one traveler, long I stood
       And looked down one as far as I could
5   To where it bent in the undergrowth;
       Then took the other, as just as fair,
       And having perhaps the better claim,
       Because it was grassy and wanted wear;
       Though as for that the passing there
10 Had worn them really about the same,
       And both that morning equally lay
       In leaves no step had trodden black.
       Oh, I kept the first for another day!
       Yet knowing how way leads on to way,
15 I doubted if I should ever come back.
       I shall be telling this with a sigh
       Somewhere ages and ages hence:
       Two roads diverged in a wood, and I—
       I took the one less travelled by,
20 And that has made all the difference.

1. What can be said about the author's tone in "The Road Not Taken"?

Ⓐ He feels some remorse about his decision.

Ⓑ He feels that he has accomplished something great.

Ⓒ He feels that his path has been different.

Ⓓ He feels that he should not have gone into the woods.

2. How does the point of view affect the tone of this poem?

Ⓐ It creates a feeling of superiority in the reader.

Ⓑ It causes the reader to feel slightly distanced from the scene.

Ⓒ It makes the reader feel as if he/she is making the same decision.

Ⓓ It causes the reader to feel as if he/she has no choice.

3. What is the main theme in this poem?

Ⓐ Deciding which road to take while on a hike

Ⓑ Making choices that may be different from others

Ⓒ How to make the best of a decision in the past

Ⓓ Wondering about the choices that others have made

4. What is the setting of this poem?

Ⓐ The early morning, near some wood in the early or late spring

Ⓑ The edges of a well-worn path near thick undergrowth

Ⓒ Two paths that are near a more traveled one in the late morning

Ⓓ The morning, in an autumnal forest with two walking paths

5. Which lines from this poem show a kind of irony?

Ⓐ 16, 17, and 20

Ⓑ 4, 5 and 6

Ⓒ 6 and 8

Ⓓ 18 and 19

Read the following passage from Heywood Broun's <u>The Fifty-First Dragon</u> to answer questions 6-10:

> OF all the pupils at the knight school Gawaine le Cœur-Hardy was among the least promising. He was tall and sturdy, but his instructors soon discovered that he lacked spirit. He would hide in the woods when the jousting class was called, although his companions and members of the faculty sought to appeal to his better nature by shouting to him to come out and break his neck like a man. Even when they told him that the lances were padded, the horses no more than ponies and the field unusually soft for late autumn, Gawaine refused to grow enthusiastic. The Headmaster and the Assistant Professor of Pleasaunce were discussing the case one spring afternoon and the Assistant Professor could see no remedy but expulsion.
>
> "No," said the Headmaster, as he looked out at the purple hills which ringed the school, "I think I'll train him to slay dragons."
>
> "He might be killed," objected the Assistant Professor.
>
> "So he might," replied the Headmaster brightly, but he added, more soberly, "we must consider the greater good. We are responsible for the formation of this lad's character."

"Are the dragons particularly bad this year?" interrupted the Assistant Professor. This was characteristic. He always seemed restive when the head of the school began to talk ethics and the ideals of the institution.

"I've never known them worse," replied the Headmaster. "Up in the hills to the south last week they killed a number of peasants, two cows and a prize pig. And if this dry spell holds there's no telling when they may start a forest fire simply by breathing around indiscriminately."

"Would any refund on the tuition fee be necessary in case of an accident to young Cœur-Hardy?"

"No," the principal answered, judicially, "that's all covered in the contract. But as a matter of fact he won't be killed. Before I send him up in the hills I'm going to give him a magic word."

"That's a good idea," said the Professor. "Sometimes they work wonders."

6. What is the best way to describe Gawaine's character?

Ⓐ Fearless and excitable

Ⓑ Careless and frigid

Ⓒ Spiritual and careful

Ⓓ Cowardly and apathetic

7. What is the meaning of "his better nature"?

Ⓐ An increased sense of honesty

Ⓑ A man's ignoble ideas

Ⓒ A desire for propriety

Ⓓ A man's nobler instincts

8. How does the Headmaster put the professor at ease about Gawaine?

Ⓐ He tells him that Gawaine will only fight small dragons.

Ⓑ He assures him that Gawaine's contract has not expired.

Ⓒ He talks to him about the animals that have been killed by the dragons.

Ⓓ He mentions that Gawaine will be given a magic word.

9. What would be a good question for the Headmaster to consider?

Ⓐ Will Gawaine try hard to fight the dragons?

Ⓑ Will Gawaine want to learn about fighting dragons?

Ⓒ Will the professor let Gawaine learn about dragons?

Ⓓ Will the professor teach Gawaine to fight the dragons?

10. Suppose that Gawaine's parents have him removed from the school. Would the Headmaster still want Gawaine to learn to fight dragons?

Ⓐ No, he would be happy with the tuition payment.

Ⓑ No, he would think that Gawaine would eventually return.

Ⓒ Yes, because Gawaine is naturally very tall and strong.

Ⓓ Yes, because Gawaine will get a special word for protection.

11. What might be one argument against the idea that "repetition is the mother of learning"? Write your answer below.

_____

_____

12. If you needed to write an essay supporting the idea that "repetition is the mother of learning," what could one supporting detail be?

Ⓐ Parents who repeat the same idea to their children hope that the children will eventually comprehend and understand it.

Ⓑ Studies show that children who are exposed to different environments are able to adapt better to changes.

Ⓒ Children who have heard the same topic presented in different ways show a better understanding of it.

Ⓓ Scientists have claimed that repetition of a certain idea may have some bearing on the way children look at their worlds.

13. Which of the following statements should come after the topic sentence below?
  "Video games are a part of every child's life, but scientists are now showing how damaging they may be."

Ⓐ Some guys at a research place looked at why kids totally love games and they think that it has something to do with their thought patterns.

Ⓑ Scientists got some kids to play games in a study and then told us all about it so they could show the importance of video games.

Ⓒ Children and their parents always fight about games, and scientists know it—they just had to find a way to show it.

Ⓓ In a recent study, scientists studied the brain scans of "gamers," or those who play video games regularly.

14. Write a thesis sentence for a paper titled "Safe *and* Fun: Extreme Sports"?

_____

_____

_____

15. Which of the following choices could best start an essay entitled "The Rise of the Robots: New Inventions for Everyday Life"?

Ⓐ You may not take robots for granted right now, but if scientists have their way, you soon will. A whole host of new robotic helpers is on the way. Everything from washing your floors to helping grandma take a walk could be done by a new kind of robot.

Ⓑ Robots are everywhere in science fiction, but are they soon to be an important part of life? Japanese engineers created the HRP-4C in 2009, a robot that can walk. The robot is designed to look like a young woman and can smile.

Ⓒ Robots that look like people raise a lot of very important ethical questions—many that we don't even want to consider. Robots are really just machines, but the newer ones look so much like people that they may give you pause. Do robots have rights?

Ⓓ Do you hate doing homework and taking tests? If scientists have anything to say about it, you may be able to get some help from a robot friend. The new robot tutors are designed to not only make schoolwork easier, but fun.

16. What quotation would most likely appear in a paragraph entitled "Hard Work Really *Does* Pay Off"?

Ⓐ "And to get real work experience, you need a job, and most jobs will require you to have had either real work experience or a graduate degree. " (Donald Norman)

Ⓑ "Don't go around saying the world owes you a living. The world owes you nothing. It was here first." (Mark Twain)

Ⓒ "Men for the sake of getting a living forget to live." (Margaret Fuller)

Ⓓ "O man you are busy working for the world, and the world is busy trying to turn you out." (Abu Bakr)

17. Read the sentence below. Which of the following choices should come next?
"Margie and George had known the water in the old fish tank was going to be too cold."

Ⓐ Margie had known about the fish. They were all tropical fish that could swim very well and were quite beautiful.

Ⓑ George, of course, had shown Margie the fish. They knew that the fish were different but didn't tell each other.

Ⓒ The kinds of fish that go in cool water were not cheap. The kinds of fish that go in warm water were.

Ⓓ In fact, it was so cold that it frequently cooled the house in the summer, and was certainly no place for tropical fish.

18. Which option best replaces the italicized words in the following sentence?
*"Angel **got into** her email account and read the homework message from her teacher."*

Ⓐ went on

Ⓑ signed up

Ⓒ logged into

Ⓓ got up

Read the following passage from Mark Twain's The Adventures of Tom Sawyer to answer questions 19-22:

[Tom Sawyer, a young boy who lives with his Aunt Polly, needs to whitewash the fence outside their house. Tom is not excited about spending the afternoon working hard.]

He got out his worldly wealth and examined it—bits of toys, marbles, and trash; enough to buy an exchange of WORK, maybe, but not half enough to buy so much as half an hour of pure freedom. So he returned his straitened means to his pocket, and gave up the idea of trying to buy the boys. At this dark and hopeless moment an inspiration burst upon him! Nothing less than a great, magnificent inspiration.

He took up his brush and went tranquilly to work. Ben Rogers hove in sight presently—the very boy, of all boys, whose ridicule he had been dreading. Ben's gait was the hop-skip-and-jump—proof enough that his heart was light and his anticipations high. He was eating an apple, and giving a long, melodious whoop, at intervals, followed by a deep-toned ding-dong-dong, ding-dong-dong, for he was personating a steamboat. As he drew near, he slackened speed, took the middle of the street, leaned far over to starboard and rounded to ponderously and with laborious pomp and circumstance—for he was personating the Big Missouri, and considered himself to be drawing nine feet of water. He was boat and captain and engine-bells combined, so he had to imagine himself standing on his own hurricane-deck giving the orders and executing them:
"Stop her, sir! Ting-a-ling-ling!" The headway ran almost out, and he drew up slowly toward the sidewalk.

"Ship up to back! Ting-a-ling-ling!" His arms straightened and stiffened down his sides.

"Set her back on the stabboard! Ting-a-ling-ling! Chow! ch-chow-wow! Chow!" His right hand, mean-time, describing stately circles—for it was representing a forty-foot wheel.

"Let her go back on the labboard! Ting-a-ling-ling! Chow-ch-chow-chow!" The left hand began to describe circles.

"Stop the stabboard! Ting-a-ling-ling! Stop the labboard! Come ahead on the stabboard! Stop her! Let your outside turn over slow! Ting-a-ling- ling! Chow-ow-ow! Get out that head-line! LIVELY now! Come—out with your spring-line—what're you about there! Take a turn round that stump with the bight of it! Stand by that stage, now—let her go! Done with the engines, sir! Ting-a-ling-ling!"

Tom went on whitewashing—paid no attention to the steamboat. Ben stared a moment and then said: "Hi-YI! **YOU'RE up a stump, ain't you!**"

No answer. Tom surveyed his last touch with the eye of an artist, then he gave his brush another gentle sweep and surveyed the result, as before. Ben ranged up alongside of him. Tom's mouth watered for the apple, but he stuck to his work. Ben said:

"Hello, old chap, you got to work, hey?"

Tom wheeled suddenly and said:

"Why, it's you, Ben! I warn't noticing."

"Say—I'm going in a-swimming, I am. Don't you wish you could? But of course you'd druther WORK—wouldn't you? Course you would!"

Tom contemplated the boy a bit, and said:

"What do you call work?"

"Why, ain't THAT work?"

Tom resumed his whitewashing, and answered carelessly:

"Well, maybe it is, and maybe it ain't. All I know, is, it suits Tom Sawyer."

"Oh come, now, you don't mean to let on that you LIKE it?"

The brush continued to move.
"Like it? Well, I don't see why I oughtn't to like it. Does a boy get a chance to whitewash a fence every day?"

That put the thing in a new light. Ben stopped nibbling his apple. Tom swept his brush daintily back and forth—stepped back to note the effect—added a touch here and there—criticized the effect again—Ben watching every move and getting more and more interested, more and more absorbed. Presently he said:

"Say, Tom, let ME whitewash a little."

Tom considered, was about to consent; but he altered his mind:

"No—no—I reckon it wouldn't hardly do, Ben. You see, Aunt Polly's awful particular about this fence—right here on the street, you know—but if it was the back fence I wouldn't mind and SHE wouldn't. Yes, she's awful particular about this fence; it's got to be done very careful; I reckon there ain't one boy in a thousand, maybe two thousand, that can do it the way it's got to be done."

"No—is that so? Oh come, now—lemme just try. Only just a little—I'd let YOU, if you was me, Tom."
"Ben, I'd like to, honest injun; but Aunt Polly—well, Jim wanted to do it, but she wouldn't let him; Sid wanted to do it, and she wouldn't let Sid. Now don't you see how I'm fixed? If you was to tackle this fence and anything was to happen to it—"

"Oh, shucks, I'll be just as careful. Now lemme try. Say—I'll give you the core of my apple."

"Well, here—No, Ben, now don't. I'm afeard—"

"I'll give you ALL of it!"

- 128 -

Tom gave up the brush with reluctance in his face, but alacrity in his heart. And while the late steamer Big Missouri worked and sweated in the sun, the retired artist sat on a barrel in the shade close by, dangled his legs, munched his apple, and planned the slaughter of more innocents. There was no lack of material; boys happened along every little while; they came to jeer, but remained to whitewash.

19. What is the main idea in the above selection?

Ⓐ How Tom tricked others into doing his work.

Ⓑ How Tom managed to get "wealthier" off his friends.

Ⓒ How Tom finished the house painting in one afternoon.

Ⓓ How Tom taught others about the value of work.

20. According to the passage, Ben says, "YOU'RE up a stump, ain't you!" Which of the following choices reflects a better way to express this sentence?

Ⓐ "You're in a lot of trouble, are you?"

Ⓑ "Your in trouble, aren't you?"

Ⓒ "Your in a lot of trouble, ain't ya?"

Ⓓ "You're in trouble, aren't you?"

21. Read the paragraph from the text and answer the question that follows.

Tom swept his brush daintily back and forth—stepped back to note the effect—added a touch here and there—criticized the effect again—Ben watching every move and getting more and more interested, more and more absorbed.

Which word is a synonym for daintily?

Ⓐ delicately

Ⓑ furiously

Ⓒ roughly

Ⓓ vigorously

22. Read the excerpt from the text below and answer the question that follows.

Tom surveyed his last touch with the eye of an artist, then he gave his brush another gentle sweep and surveyed the result, as before.

Select the answer that best defines the word "surveyed".

Ⓐ rubbed on

Ⓑ looked over

Ⓒ redid

Ⓓ complained about

Read the following passage from Douglas Fairbanks's <u>Live and Laugh</u> to answer questions 23-27:

There is one thing in this good old world that is positively sure—happiness is for all who strive to be happy—and those who laugh are happy.

Everybody is eligible—you—me—the other fellow.

Happiness is fundamentally a state of mind—not a state of body.

And mind controls.

Indeed it is possible to stand with one foot on the inevitable "banana peel" of life with both eyes peering into the Great Beyond, and still be happy, comfortable, and serene—if we will even so much as smile.
It's all a state of mind, I tell you—and I'm sure of what I say. That's why I have taken up my fountain pen. I want to talk to my friends—you hosts of people who have written to me for my recipe. In moving pictures all I can do is act my part and grin for you. What I say is a matter of your own inference, but with my pen I have a means of getting around the "silent drama" which prevents us from organizing a "close-up" with one another.

In starting I'm going to ask you "foolish question number 1."—

Do you ever laugh?

I mean do you ever laugh right out—spontaneously—just as if the police weren't listening with drawn clubs and a finger on the button connecting with the "hurry-up" wagon? Well, if you don't, you should. Start off the morning with a laugh and you needn't worry about the rest of the day.

<u>I like to laugh. It is a tonic. It braces me up—makes me feel fine!—and keeps me in prime mental condition. Laughter is a physiological necessity. The nerve system requires it. The deep, forceful chest movement in itself sets the blood to racing thereby livening up the circulation—which is good for us. Perhaps you hadn't thought of that? Perhaps you didn't realize that laughing automatically re-oxygenates the blood—your blood—and keeps it red? It does all of that, and besides, it relieves the tension from your brain.</u>

Real laughter is spontaneous. Like water from the spring it bubbles forth a creation of mingled action and spontaneity—two magic potions in themselves—the very essence of laughter—the unrestrained emotion within us!

So, for me, it is to laugh! Why not stick along? The experiment won't hurt you. All we need is will power, and that is a personal matter for each individual to seek and acquire for himself. Many of us already possess it, but many of us do not.

Take the average man on the street for example. Watch him go plodding along—no **spring**, no elasticity, no vim. He is in check-rein—how can he laugh when his **pep** is all gone and the sand in his craw isn't there any more? What he needs is spirit! Energy—the power to force himself into action! For him there is no hope unless he will take up physical training in some form that will put him in normal physical condition—after that everything simplifies itself. The brain responds to the new blood in circulation and thus the mental processes are ready to make a fight against the inertia of stagnation which has held them in bondage.

23. What supports the author's premise that "happiness is… a state of mind"?

Ⓐ Spontaneous laughter is useful.

Ⓑ Those who try to be happy are happy.

Ⓒ People should consider the "average man on the street."

Ⓓ Physical exercise is needed for unenthusiastic people.

24. Which of the following is the best summary of the above selection?

Ⓐ The mind is very important for determining happiness, and laughter is an important part of being happy.

Ⓑ The mind controls the body, so if you can laugh about something every day, you will find that your blood circulation improves.

Ⓒ The average person is interested in knowing how Douglas Fairbanks stays so positive, and he has written about how staying healthy is vital.

Ⓓ Average people do not feel happy because they do not try to laugh or see things in a different way.

25. Read the paragraph below.

I like to laugh. It is a tonic. It braces me up—makes me feel fine!—and keeps me in prime mental condition. Laughter is a physiological necessity. The nerve system requires it. The deep, forceful chest movement in itself sets the blood to racing thereby livening up the circulation—which is good for us. Perhaps you hadn't thought of that? Perhaps you didn't realize that laughing automatically re-oxygenates the blood—your blood—and keeps it red? It does all of that, and besides, it relieves the tension from your brain.

What does the author compare laughter to in the text?

_____

26. Which of the following is closest in meaning to the word "pep"?

Ⓐ Enterprise

Ⓑ Apathy

Ⓒ Liveliness

Ⓓ Lethargy

27. Which of the following is closest in meaning to the word "spring," as used in the above selection?

Ⓐ A season that follows the winter

Ⓑ A sudden motion

Ⓒ A violent change of mood

Ⓓ A bounce

28. Which of the following introduces a claim that is not sufficiently supported by the evidence?

Ⓐ That's why I have taken up my fountain pen.

Ⓑ Take the average man on the street for example.

Ⓒ Start off the morning with a laugh and you needn't worry about the rest of the day.

Ⓓ Why not stick along? The experiment won't hurt you.

29. Which of the following would be the word that means "the study of the earth, its history, and its surface"?

Ⓐ Geocaching

Ⓑ Geography

Ⓒ Geology

Ⓓ Geometrics

30. According to the statement below, which of the following choices best matches the meaning of the underlined word?

"The prince set two guards to cover the first watch, knowing that the enemy might come at any hour."

Ⓐ A small device used to determine time

Ⓑ To observe carefully

Ⓒ A period of time for surveillance

Ⓓ To wait on attentively

31. Which of the following dialogues best develop the action and characters in the story?

Ⓐ Jane: "Ouch! I told you not to leave the cabinet door open! Now look what's happened—again! My other knee is cut now."
Peter: "It's your own fault. If you were paying attention, it wouldn't happen. Besides, who told you to go in there? Nosey, are we?"

Ⓑ Jane: "Ouch! That really hurt! I can't believe that it happened again. It's like the same things over and over again."
Peter: "Well, it's really your own fault. I don't see how it has to do with someone else. You really need to be more careful."

Ⓒ Jane: "Ouch! Why is that cabinet door open again! I thought I closed it yesterday. As a matter of fact, I am sure that I closed it yesterday."
Peter: "You probably just forgot to do it. After all, you are pretty absent-minded."

Ⓓ Jane: "Ouch! Did you leave that cabinet door open? I just hit my knee on it and now I have a big cut there. It really hurts!"
Peter: "Is your knee hurt? Why aren't you more careful? Now both of your knees are cut."

32. Which of the following sentences probably comes next?
"First, Janice rolled up her sleeves and glanced at the clock."

Ⓐ She counted backwards two hours establishing the starting point for her story.

Ⓑ Finally, she counted backwards two hours to establish the starting point for her story.

Ⓒ Second, she was counting backwards for two hours to establish the starting point in her story.

Ⓓ Then, she counted backwards two hours to establish the starting point for her story.

33. Which of the following endings could be a satisfactory conclusion to the story?
Bob and Peter went skateboarding in the park on Saturday, even though it was supposed to rain. The boys had been skating for a few hours when the rumble of thunder sounded and raindrops began to fall. The boys gathered up their boards and were running towards the park exit when they heard a cry. "Help! My brother has fallen in the water and I can't reach him! Help! He can't swim!" Bob pulled Peter's sleeve and pointed towards the pond. A frightened girl ran back and forth by the edge of the water.

Ⓐ Bob and Peter take their skateboards home and call the police to see if they can help the boy in the park.

Ⓑ Bob and Peter go skateboarding around the pond to see if the boy is really in trouble before heading home.

Ⓒ Bob goes home while Peter goes to the pond to see if the girl needs some help. He tries to rescue the boy from the pond.

Ⓓ Bob and Peter go to the pond to help the boy. They use their skateboards to help pull the boy from the water.

34. Which of the following sentences is written correctly?

Ⓐ Peter and Jaime slowly opened the door peered into the shadows and then ran across the room.

Ⓑ Peter and Jaime slowly opened the door, peered into the shadows, and then ran across the room.

Ⓒ Peter and Jaime slowly opened the door, peered into the shadows, and then ran across the room

Ⓓ Peter and Jaime, slowly opened the door, peered into the shadows, and then ran across the room.

35. Come up with a word that would fit in the blank.

"Of all the puppies in the kennel, James chose the chubbiest one. He didn't even look at the dogs who were _____ and underfed. He had no interest in a sickly animal."

---

36. Pretend you read an article in a science journal that showed organic food is healthier than non-organic food. One of your classmates, Charlie, then said organic food is not healthier for you. Which of the following statements could you make in a group discussion on this topic?

Ⓐ "Although Charlie disagrees, I believe organic food is healthier for you than non-organic food because of a research article I read in a science journal."

Ⓑ "I believe that organic food is healthier for you than non-organic food is, but Charlie says otherwise."

Ⓒ "Even though Charlie says that organic food is not healthier for you than other foods, I think that his conclusion is based on his own opinion."

Ⓓ "Charlie mentioned that he does not believe that organic food is healthier for you than other kinds of food, but it's quite obvious that he is guilty of an *ad hominem* attack."

37. Which part of the sentence is the infinitive?

"To persevere in the face of hardship shows great character."

Ⓐ face of hardship

Ⓑ in the face of

Ⓒ To persevere

Ⓓ shows great character

38. Which of the following sentences contains an error in grammar usage or punctuation?

Ⓐ My best friend, Xavier, went fishing on Saturday and hiking with his family on Sunday.

Ⓑ Angelina and Ruby, were excited about there new clothes; they decided to wear them.

Ⓒ Mr. Johnson saw the reaction in the test tube; he added more sodium to see what would happen next.

Ⓓ Sabina, frightened out of her wits, picked up the phone and dialed 9-1-1.

39. Susan is revising a research paper that she wrote for English class. She decided that the underlined words below are too informal.

> We should all remember the sacrifices that have been made to ensure our freedoms, and we should take full advantage of those freedoms. If we don't, those who died to ensure that all Americans have the right to life, liberty, and the pursuit of happiness will have died in vain. I hope that my <u>age group</u> will be the first of many to make voting one of our most important and treasured rights once again.

Rewrite the third sentence, replacing the underlined words with a more formal term.

_____

_____

_____

40. The following sentence contains an error.

> If people do not stand up and choose their own leaders, someone else will do it for them: and who knows what those leaders will stand for?

Rewrite the sentence below, correcting the error.

_____

_____

_____

Answers and Explanations

1. A: Line 16 reveals that the author will be talking about this moment later with a sigh. There is nothing in the poem to indicate that the author has done something great or that he should have not gone into the woods. While he does seem to say that his path has been different than others, that does not describe the tone of the poem.

2. C: The first person point of view makes the reader feel as if he/she is involved in making the same decision. The other choices involve other points of view: an omniscient reader would feel superior or even a little distanced from the scene. The reader also has a clear choice, so letter D would not be a good selection.

3. B: This is because the writer mentions there are two paths, and one seemed more worn than the other, showing it was more often used by travelers. The other choices involve reading too much into the poem.

4. D: The setting is laid out in lines 1 and 11.

5. A: Frost uses a type of irony called "verbal irony" here, and shows us his feelings by using expressions that go against what the literal words say.

6. D: Gawaine is said to be tall and sturdy, but would run away and hide at the smallest sign of trouble.

7. D: "His better nature" is a common way of talking about a person's deeper character.

8. D: Letter A is not mentioned in the text, and the other choices do not directly answer the question.

9. B: Considering Gawaine's character, this is the only choice that makes sense because it is well known that Gawaine is cowardly and the professor doesn't seem to know much about dragons.

10. A: This can be inferred from the text:
"Would any refund on the tuition fee be necessary in case of an accident to young Cœur-Hardy?"
"No," the principal answered, judicially, "that's all covered in the contract."

11. "Just saying something over and over again doesn't mean that a student really understands it." This statement is one possible example, as it supports a counter-argument in a clear manner.

12. C: While the other choices may be supporting details, this is the best choice because it is most closely related to the main topic.

13. D: This choice makes the most sense because the topic sentence involves how scientists are showing that video games are bad for children.

14. "Extreme sports like snowboarding, skateboarding, and mountain climbing can all be done in a safe and exciting manner." This would be one example of a good thesis statement for a paragraph about "Safe *and* Fun: Extreme Sports".

15. A: This is the only choice that directly reflects all aspects of the essay's title.

16. B: The other choices may mention work, but they do not support the idea that hard work is good and profitable.

17. D: This is the only choice that correctly uses a transition and addresses every part of the first sentence and provides new information for creating a story.

18. C: This bit of computer jargon refers to someone signing into or gaining access to their email account or profile page on the Internet.

19. A: This is one of Twain's most oft-repeated passages, and while the other choices are true, they are not giving a good summary of the paragraphs.

20. D: This sentence shows how the quote should be written. The other selections all involve grammar errors.

21. A: Tom was painting daintily or delicately. These words are synonyms and both describe him painting in an easy, gentle pattern.

22. B: In this sentence, Tom was looking over his work with the eye of an artist.

23. B: This is the only statement that directly gives support to the idea that "mind over matter" is a part of the will. The other choices are points from the paragraph used to illustrate other ideas.

24. A: While all of the choices have some truth to them, this is the only one that gives a complete summary of the selection.

25. He compares it to a tonic. This is directly stated in the text: "I like to laugh. It is a tonic. It braces me up..."

26. C: "Liveliness" is another word for pep. Enterprise refers to an endeavor, apathy is indifference, and lethargy is sluggishness.

27. D: While the other choices may have something to do with the word "spring," they do not give the correct definition for the word as it is used in the selection.

28. C: The other choices either do not make a specific claim, or make a claim that the author tries to support. There is no support to show that the reader won't have to worry about the rest of the day.

29. C: "Geo" is the Greek prefix for "Earth" and "-logy" is a suffix meaning "the study or discourse."

30. C: The other choices are other meanings for the word "watch," but option C is the only choice that makes sense in the context of the sentence.

31. A: This choice provides the best character and story development.

32. D: The other choices do not use the transition words correctly nor follow the pattern set in the first sentence.

33. D: Based on the boys' behavior in the story, this is the only choice that makes sense. Bob and Peter are not afraid to take risks (they go to the park despite warnings of rain) and they stop to listen to the cries for help.

34. B: This shows the clearest expression of the main idea and is grammatically correct.

35. A good word to go in the blank would be "skinny", or any synonym of skinny.

36. A: This choice acknowledges your classmate's ideas while explaining and supporting your own claims in a polite fashion.

37. C: This is the infinitive, which is simply the basic form of a verb.

38. B: This sentence is incorrect because it has the wrong word for "their" (there). It also has a misplaced comma (after "Ruby").

39. A more precise word for "age group" would be "generation".

40. C: This sentence has two independent clauses that include "and" as the coordinating conjunction. Adding a comma between "them" and "and" is the most appropriate change to make the meaning of the sentence clear. A semicolon or a colon would not be correct here, and would cause the reader to be confused. The corrected sentence would read:

If people do not stand up and choose their own leaders, someone else will do it for them, and who knows what those leaders will stand for?

English Language Arts Practice Test #2

Practice Questions

1. Which of the following is similar to the claim made by Albert Einstein that "Sometimes one pays most for the things one gets for nothing"?

Ⓐ "The best things in life are free."

Ⓑ "Easy come, easy go."

Ⓒ "There's no such thing as a free lunch."

Ⓓ "A stitch in time saves nine."

2. Which of the following best provides detailed support for the claim that "seatbelts save lives"?

Ⓐ A government website containing driving accident information

Ⓑ A blog developed by one of the largest car companies in the world

Ⓒ An encyclopedia entry on the seatbelt and its development

Ⓓ An instant message sent out by a famous race car driver

3. Which of the following choices best completes the sentence below?
It is better to see the doctor for routine, yearly check-ups instead of waiting until you are experiencing a big health problem _____.

Ⓐ After which the doctor may be able to provide a referral to a specialist.

Ⓑ Because the doctor can usually spot problems before they get too big to handle.

Ⓒ Since a routine visit is more likely to happen at least once a year.

Ⓓ So the best thing to do is to contact your doctor when you need help.

4. Which of the following would best support the argument that people cause global climate change?

Ⓐ The average global temperature has increased 1.5 degrees Fahrenheit since 1880.

Ⓑ Common greenhouse gases include carbon dioxide and water vapor.

Ⓒ Most of the greenhouse gases today come from burning things like coal and other fossil fuels for energy.

Ⓓ The average person breathes out about 1.0 kg of carbon dioxide every day, while the average cow produces about 80 kg of methane.

5. Write a good concluding sentence for a paragraph entitled "The Best Books You've Never Read"?

_____

_____

_____

6. Which of the following choices would be the best beginning for an essay on "Scientists Debate: Global Climate Change"?

Ⓐ The Earth is heating up. The polar ice caps are melting and whole species are going extinct while governments and scientists argue over rules and regulations.

Ⓑ The argument seems to be about whether climate change is really happening and if so, who causes it. Some scientists argue that people are causing the change.

Ⓒ If the Earth heats up, what will our new world look like? Scientists who have dedicated their lives to understanding climate change have projected a series of scenarios that could happen.

Ⓓ While few people can understand all of the issues related to climate change, one thing is sure: scientists do not agree. There seem to be several different views on how to look at climate change data.

7. Fill in the blank with the correct transitional phrase in the following passage?

_However, not all scientists agree that people are causing climate change.
_____, the famous "Hockey Stick" graph, which showed a huge spike in the global temperature, is being debated._

_____

8. Which of the following words best replaces the underlined term?

Newer "green" products are available, such as recycled boxes, non-toxic baby toys, and cloth grocery bags.

Ⓐ plant-based

Ⓑ garden-like

Ⓒ environmentally-friendly

Ⓓ climate-altered

9. Which sentence best completes the following paragraph?

There are many issues our school faces. First, there is a problem with litter. Students do not seem concerned about the garbage and paper they leave on the floors and desks. Second, there are issues with the class schedules. Students have to run from one end of the campus to the other in just a few minutes. Finally, the library does not have enough money to buy books. All of the money for the library had to be used to fix the water damage from the storm.

Ⓐ The worst of these three problems is the issue with litter, since class schedules and library problems are not as serious.

Ⓑ These three problems are the most serious issues that need to be addressed because they affect the daily operation of the school.

Ⓒ The day-to-day operations of our school will be affected if we do not address one of these problems.

Ⓓ Litter, class schedules, and library problems all contribute to the problems our school is facing, and they are quite serious.

Read the following selection from H. G. Well's book, The Time Machine, to answer questions 10-13:

[The Time Traveller is talking to his friends. He has just explained that while three dimensions—length, breadth, and thickness— are typically accepted, a "fourth dimension" should also be considered.]

'Well, I do not mind telling you I have been at work upon this geometry of Four Dimensions for some time. **Some of my results are curious.** For instance, here is a portrait of a man at eight years old, another at fifteen, another at seventeen, another at twenty-three, and so on. All these are evidently sections, as it were, Three-Dimensional representations of his Four-Dimensioned being, which is a fixed and unalterable thing.

'Scientific people,' proceeded the Time Traveller, after the pause required for the proper assimilation of this, 'know very well that Time is only a kind of Space. Here is a popular scientific diagram, a weather record. This line I trace with my finger shows the movement of the barometer. Yesterday it was so high, yesterday night it fell, then this morning it rose again, and so gently upward to here. Surely the mercury did not trace this line in any of the dimensions of Space generally recognized? But certainly it traced such a line, and that line, therefore, we must conclude was along the Time-Dimension.'

'But,' said the Medical Man, staring hard at a coal in the fire, 'if Time is really only a fourth dimension of Space, why is it, and why has it always been, regarded as something different? And why cannot we move in Time as we move about in the other dimensions of Space?'

The Time Traveller smiled. 'Are you sure we can move freely in Space? Right and left we can go, backward and forward freely enough, and men always

- 142 -

have done so. I admit we move freely in two dimensions. But how about up and down? Gravitation limits us there.'

'Not exactly,' said the Medical Man. **'There are balloons.'**

'But before the balloons, save for spasmodic jumping and the inequalities of the surface, man had no freedom of vertical movement.'

'Still they could move a little up and down,' said the Medical Man.

'Easier, far easier down than up.'

'And you cannot move at all in Time, you cannot get away from the present moment.'

'My dear sir, that is just where you are wrong. That is just where the whole world has gone wrong..."

10. Which of the following best summarizes the above selection?

Ⓐ It is a conversation involving the age of men and space.

Ⓑ It is a conversation about the nature of time and space.

Ⓒ It is a dialogue from two friends about their medical ideas.

Ⓓ It is a dialogue from two colleagues about time and distance.

11. As referred to in paragraph 6 above, what is a synonym for the word "spasmodic"?

_____

12. In this question, you will need to compare the paragraph that appears in question 10 (about school issues) to the selection from The Time Machine above. How do the structures of the texts contribute to their functions? Choose the best answer.

Ⓐ The Time Machine text uses dialogue to pull the reader along to a conclusion, while the straight-forward listing of issues in question 10 keeps the reader's focus by being short and to the point.

Ⓑ The Time Machine text uses an explanation of gravity to interest the reader, while the straight-forward listing of issues in question 10 keeps the reader's focus by explaining some solutions.

Ⓒ The Time Machine text is short and comes to the point, while the listing of issues in question 10 allows for the reader to think more deeply about the ideas.

Ⓓ The Time Machine text uses complex arguments to make a simple point, while the straight-forward listing of issues in question 10 does not allow for the development of arguments.

13. What effect does the point-of-view in this story have on its development?

Ⓐ It makes the reader feel intelligent.

Ⓑ It creates confusion.

Ⓒ It builds suspense.

Ⓓ It develops a feeling of contentment.

Read the passage below from How it Works by Archibald Williams to answer questions 14-17:

The most familiar form of electricity is that known as magnetism. When a bar of steel or iron is magnetized, it is supposed that the molecules in it turn and arrange themselves with all their north-seeking poles towards the one end of the bar, and their south-seeking poles towards the other. If the bar is balanced freely on a pivot, it comes to rest pointing north and south; for, the earth being a huge magnet, its north pole attracts all the north-seeking poles of the molecules, and its south poles the south-seeking poles. (The north-seeking pole of a magnet is marked N., though it is in reality the south pole; for unlike poles are mutually attractive, and like poles repellent.)

There are two forms of magnet—permanent and temporary. If steel is magnetized, it remains so; but soft iron loses practically all its magnetism as soon as the cause of magnetization is withdrawn. This is what we should expect; for steel is more closely **compacted** than iron, and the molecules therefore would be able to turn about more easily. It is fortunate for us that this is so, since on the rapid magnetization and demagnetization of soft iron depends the action of many of our _____ mechanisms.

14. Which of the following words best completes the blank?

Ⓐ molecular

Ⓑ north-seeking

Ⓒ pole-like

Ⓓ electrical

15. Which of the following is closest in meaning to the word "compacted" in the above selection?

Ⓐ Pledge

Ⓑ Efficient

Ⓒ Compress

Ⓓ Dense

16. What might be the best way to help students understand the concept of magnetism?

Ⓐ Have them read the encyclopedia entry on temporary magnets and permanent magnets and then ask students to write an essay on the topic.

Ⓑ Ask students a series of discussion questions related to electricity and then ask them how they would explain it to others.

Ⓒ Show them a short movie that demonstrates the movement of the molecules in a piece of magnetized metal and then have students participate in group discussions.

Ⓓ Allow students to examine a graphic illustrating the electro-magnetic spectrum and draw conclusions about magnetism based on the graphic representation.

17. Which of the following sentences best develops the idea of how magnetism can be tested?

Ⓐ If steel is magnetized, it remains so; but soft iron loses practically all its magnetism as soon as the cause of magnetization is withdrawn.

Ⓑ The most familiar form of electricity is that known as magnetism.

Ⓒ When a bar of steel or iron is magnetized, it is supposed that the molecules in it turn and arrange themselves with all their north-seeking poles towards the one end of the bar, and their south-seeking poles towards the other.

Ⓓ If the bar is balanced freely on a pivot, it comes to rest pointing north and south; for, the earth being a huge magnet, its north pole attracts all the north-seeking poles of the molecules, and its south poles the south-seeking poles.

Read the following statements to answer questions 18 and 19:

> Lisa Grant: "Schools should make students wear uniforms. Everyone would look the same. Students would be able to respect each other based on their ideas and character because they would no longer be judged by their appearance."
>
> Joe Smith: "Students should not have to wear uniforms. Clothing is an important part of self-expression. Taking away that method of expression is suppressing that student's rights."

18. What idea do both of the students seem to agree upon?

_____

_____

_____

19. Which of the following statements could NOT provide support for BOTH arguments?

Ⓐ A number of local school districts have recently implemented dress codes.

Ⓑ School administrators have been in talks with parents over the issue of uniforms.

Ⓒ Students have reported that school uniforms are costly and typically ill-fitting.

Ⓓ Several groups of students have been organized to discuss uniform dress codes.

Read the following selection from Ten American Girls From History *by Kate Dickinson Sweetser to answer questions 20-23:*

[Clara has begun her work of ministering to soldiers on the front lines of the civil war. Her tireless efforts and care have taken her to some of the most horrific battles of the war]

Clara Barton!—Only the men who lay wounded or dying on the battle-field knew the thrill and the comfort that the name carried. Again and again her life was in danger—once at Antietam, when stooping to give a drink of water to an injured boy, a bullet whizzed between them. It ended the life of **the poor lad**, but only tore a hole in Clara Barton's sleeve. And so, again and again, it seemed as if a special Providence protected her from death or injury. At Fredericksburg, when the dead, starving and wounded lay frozen on the ground, and there was no effective organization for proper relief, with swift, silent efficiency Clara Barton moved among them, having the snow cleared away and under the banks finding famished, frozen figures which were once men. She rushed to have an old chimney torn down and built fire-blocks, over which she soon had kettles full of coffee and gruel steaming.

As she was bending over a wounded rebel, he whispered to her: "Lady, you have been kind to me ... every street of the city is covered by our cannon. When your entire army has reached the other side of the Rappahannock, they will find Fredericksburg only a slaughter-pen. Not a regiment will escape. Do not go over, for you will go to certain death."

She thanked him for the kindly warning and later told of the call that came to her to go across the river, and what happened. She says:

"At ten o'clock of the battle day when the rebel fire was hottest, the shells rolling down every street, and the bridge under the heavy cannonade, a courier dashed over, and, rushing up the steps of the house where I was, placed in my hand a crumpled, bloody piece of paper, a request from the lion-hearted old surgeon on the opposite shore, establishing his hospitals in the very jaws of death:

"'Come to me,' he wrote. 'Your place is here.'

"The faces of the rough men working at my side, which eight weeks before had flushed with indignation at the thought of being controlled by a woman, grew ashy white as they guessed the nature of the summons, ... and they begged me to send them, but save myself. I could only allow them to go with me if they chose, and in twenty minutes we were rocking across the swaying bridge, the water hissing with shot on either side.

"Over into that city of death, its roofs riddled by shell, its every church a crowded hospital, every street a battle-line, every hill a rampart, every rock a fortress, and every stone wall a blazing line of forts.

"Oh, what a day's work was that! How those long lines of blue, rank on rank, charged over the open acres, up to the very mouths of those blazing guns, and how like grain before the sickle they fell and melted away.

"An officer stepped to my side to assist me over the débris at the end of the bridge. While our hands were raised in the act of stepping down, a piece of an exploding shell hissed through between us, just below our arms, carrying away a portion of both the skirts of his coat and my dress, rolling along the ground a few rods from us like a harmless pebble in the water. The next instant a solid shot thundered over our heads, a noble steed bounded in the air and with his gallant rider rolled in the dirt not thirty feet in the rear. Leaving the kind-hearted officer, I passed on alone to the hospital. In less than a half-hour he was brought to me—dead."

She was passing along a street in the heart of the city when she had to step aside to let a regiment of infantry march by. At that moment General Patrick saw her, and, thinking she was a frightened resident of the city who had been left behind in the general exodus, leaned from his saddle and said, reassuringly:

"You are alone and in great danger, madam. Do you want protection?"

With a rare smile, Miss Barton said, as she looked at the ranks of soldiers, "Thank you, but I think I am the best-protected woman in the United States."

20. What can be inferred from the fact that the men's faces turned "white" in the underlined sentence?

Ⓐ The men were afraid that Clara would be seriously hurt or killed by going to help.

Ⓑ The men had not wanted Clara to tend to them or order them around when she first arrived.

Ⓒ The men were terrified of the coming war and wanted Clara to escape with them.

Ⓓ The men did not want to be moved to the hospital on the other side of the bridge.

21. Which of the following might be a good title for the above selection?

Ⓐ Clara Barton: "The Angel of the Battlefields"

Ⓑ "The Angel of the Civil War"

Ⓒ Civil War Nurses and the Work of Clara Barton

Ⓓ "When the Fighting Was Over: Clara Barton, Civil War Hero"

22. Why does the author mention the instances when Clara's life had been in danger on the battlefield?

Ⓐ To show that Clara was an unwilling participant in the initial war effort.

Ⓑ To help the reader picture how Clara seemed to not really be a part of the battle.

Ⓒ To compare how many battles she lived through with how many armed men had not.

Ⓓ To illustrate how battles were turned through the care she provided.

23. Which of the following best explains why the author referred to one of the soldiers as "the poor lad"?

Ⓐ She wanted to show that the man had little or no material belongings.

Ⓑ She wanted to build sympathy for the young man who died.

Ⓒ She wanted to show that the soldier had only been a young boy, not a man.

Ⓓ She wanted to create an image in the mind of the reader about the soldier.

24. Which of the following choices is closest in meaning to the sentence below?
[Mercutio, Romeo's friend, utters this line shortly after receiving a fatal wound in this selection from William Shakespeare's Romeo and Juliet.]

"Ask for me tomorrow and you shall find me a grave man."
Act III, scene i: lines 97 – 98

Ⓐ If you question about me tomorrow, you can see that I am not being silly.

Ⓑ Please ask about my tomb tomorrow when you visit.

Ⓒ I am very serious about this issue, so please come and see me tomorrow.

Ⓓ I will not survive this incident and will be dead by tomorrow.

25. The following definition is from the dictionary. According to this definition, what part of speech goes with the part of the definition "one chosen or set apart"?

> *[From Chambers's Twentieth Century Dictionary (part 2 of 4: E-M), by Various]*
>
> **Elect**, *e-lekt', v.t. to choose out: to select for any office or purpose: to select by vote.—adj. chosen: taken by preference from among others: chosen for an office but not yet in it (almost always after the noun, as 'consul elect').—n. one chosen or set apart.—n.* **Elec'tion**, *the act of electing or choosing: the public choice of a person for office, usually by the votes of a constituent body: freewill: (theol.) the exercise of God's sovereign will in the predetermination of certain persons to salvation: (B.) those who are elected*

---

26. Which of the following choices would be the best way to start a paragraph about a teenager in a futuristic society?

Ⓐ M'ze looked at all of the robots in the street. Each one looked exactly the same as the other. M'ze sighed and pressed a button nearby. The Servicebots began to disappear as he rose higher into the sky.

Ⓑ M'ze gazed out moodily over the rows of mechanical Servicebots. He pressed the button on his jet pack and rose above the mob to join the flock of workers already in the skies above. "It's time to go to work," he sighed, his mind turning to his mother's tiny hospital cubicle.

Ⓒ M'ze blew his hair out of his eyes again and let his gaze fall on the rows and rows of robots before him. "Servicebots. 'Servicebots to serve you!'" he sneered at the soundless, sightless mass. He pressed a button on his jet pack.

Ⓓ M'ze thought about the robots. The Servicebots were lined up in front of him like an army. "If only my mom could see me now. She would be really disappointed." M'ze pressed a button nearby. If you saw him, you would have thought of a thin, blue bird with sad eyes.

27. Mary Shelley's _Frankenstein_ begins with a story about a young man on a journey and his subsequent meeting with Dr. Frankenstein. The same kind of technique is also used in Emily Bronte's <u>Wuthering Heights</u>. What kind of narrative technique does this represent?

Ⓐ Narrative hook

Ⓑ Deus ex machina

Ⓒ Cut-up technique

Ⓓ Frame narrative

28. Which of the following choices best fill the empty blanks in the sentences below?

> _____, Darwin did not have access to all the startling facts we do today. _____, he didn't know about DNA, which was discovered in 1953. Secondly, he did not have access to the large number of well-researched materials modern science offers."

Ⓐ "Chiefly" and "As a result"

Ⓑ "Although not likely" and "In the first place"

Ⓒ "Although this may be true" and "Serendipitously"

Ⓓ "In consideration of this" and "Firstly"

Read the following passage from Charles Dickens's David Copperfield *to answer questions 29 and 30:*

> I was born at Blunderstone, in Suffolk, or 'there by', as they say in Scotland. I was a posthumous child. My father's eyes had closed upon the light of this world six months, when mine opened on it. There is something strange to me, even now, in the reflection that he never saw me; and something stranger yet in the shadowy remembrance that I have of my first childish associations with his white grave-stone in the churchyard, and of the indefinable compassion I used to feel for it lying out alone there in the dark night, when our little parlour was warm and bright with fire and candle, and the doors of our house were—almost cruelly, it seemed to me sometimes—bolted and locked against it.

29. How does the author convey sadness?

Ⓐ Through the discussion of his birth in Scotland half a year after his father had passed away.

Ⓑ Through his description of his memories about his father's grave stone and its location.

Ⓒ Through his reflection in the mirror and his memories about his first explorations into the darkness.

Ⓓ Through his recollection that he had been born six months after his father died, and that his father had never seen his own son.

30. Which of the following could serve as a concluding sentence in the above paragraph?

Ⓐ I rarely thought of my father after I visited his grave, since his absence in my life had little to do with my future.

Ⓑ The grave stone was set in such a very lonesome place, and I couldn't bear the thought of going to visit it.

Ⓒ It was true, I missed my poor father dearly, even though I never really laid eyes on him, nor him me.

Ⓓ My father's own thoughts must have dwelt on similar issues, even though I was but a child
and he was but a specter.

31. Read the citation below. Which part of it is incorrect?
Schwartz. Michael J. What's New Is Old. New York: Classic Books, 2012.

---

32. In the book <u>Roll of Thunder, Hear My Cry</u>, the theme of independence and self-respect is one part of the story. It can be seen in the way Cassie's family interacts with others. Which of the following classic stories also has a similar theme?

Ⓐ <u>A Separate Peace</u> by John Knowles

Ⓑ <u>My Antonia</u> by Willa Cather

Ⓒ <u>The Fall of the House of Usher</u> by Edgar Allen Poe

Ⓓ <u>Wuthering Heights</u> by Emily Bronte

33. Which of the words in the sentence below is the past participle?
"Logan had already forgiven Marianne for telling his secret, and so when he was presented with a chance to treat her in kind, he simply did what he did best—he kept his mouth shut."

Ⓐ telling

Ⓑ forgiven

Ⓒ and

Ⓓ treat

34. Which of the following choices is an example of the passive voice?

(A) My friends told me about the new rules.

(B) The computers at school are much faster than the ones at the library.

(C) Her cell phone has been stolen.

(D) His hat is on the chair.

35. Which of the following sentences is written correctly?

(A) Maya, my pet bird, can say "hello" in three languages.

(B) Jason, Peter Alice and Soojin all wanted to visit the new museum.

(C) Don't forget to bring your violin—music book—and music stand to the lessons.

(D) If you bring all of the supplies for the project I will provide the workspace.

36. What word goes in the blank?

Hours of research and preparation went into the initial _____ of the computer data, and even then, the scientists called for others to investigate their claims independently.

(A) anaylsis

(B) anaylses

(C) analysis

(D) anlysis

37. What is the speaker emphasizing in this quote?

[from JFK's Inaugural Speech: 1961]
"And so, my fellow Americans, ask not what your country can do for you; ask what you can do for your country.

"My fellow citizens of the world, ask not what America will do for you, but what together we can do for the freedom of man."

(A) He's focusing on the fellowship of his countrymen.

(B) He's focusing on the freedoms of man.

(C) He's emphasizing the ability of the nation.

(D) He's emphasizing the actions of the listeners.

38. Which of the following best completes the sentence?

The dark cavern was gently illuminated by the glow from the golden cage. The heroes ventured closer to the odd light from the ancient artifact. Wen gripped his twin swords tightly as Druj raised his battle axe. The willowy sorceress, still deeply enveloped in her cloak, allowed her _____ hands to extend out from it.

(A) pale

(B) pasty

(C) cadaverous

(D) anemic

39. What might be the purpose of the following selection?

[Martin Luther King, 1963: I Have a Dream.]

Let us not wallow in the valley of despair, I say to you today, my friends.

And so even though we face the difficulties of today and tomorrow, I still have a dream. It is a dream deeply rooted in the American dream.

I have a dream that one day this nation will rise up and live out the true meaning of its creed: "We hold these truths to be self-evident, that all men are created equal."

I have a dream that one day on the red hills of Georgia, the sons of former slaves and the sons of former slave owners will be able to sit down together at the table of brotherhood.

I have a dream that one day even the state of Mississippi, a state sweltering with the heat of injustice, sweltering with the heat of oppression, will be transformed into an oasis of freedom and justice.

I have a dream that my four little children will one day live in a nation where they will not be judged by the color of their skin but by the content of their character.

I have a dream today!

(A) Instructive: To create a more positive feeling about the future of the constitution

(B) Social: To make the audience think about their own dreams and desires

(C) Commercial: To illustrate how unfair the system in Mississippi and Georgia is

(D) Political: To show how things appear to be now and what he hopes will happen

40. Which of the following sentences is correct?

Ⓐ The telescope accomplished amazing feats of enlargement, from showing the pock-marked face of the moon to the many moons of Saturn.

Ⓑ The children all said that they had the best times of their life when they all lived together in the little two-bedroom bungalow.

Ⓒ The study found that children frequently chose to use the entire bag of marshmallows for their hot cocoa.

Ⓓ The astronomers found that the planets were following regular patterns and the philosophers argue about the nature of those paths.

Answers and Explanations

1. C: This is the only answer that addresses the idea in the quote. The idea that nothing is really ever free is part of the idea Einstein was trying to communicate.

2. A: The government website would publish the most recent data on seatbelt information, like how many people wore seatbelts in the accident and how many survived. Choices B and C are more likely to be opinion-based. Choice C is tempting, but it would not give someone the most up-to-date information.

3. B: This is the best choice because it provides more information about why it is important to see the doctor for regular checkups.

4. C: This choice shows how greenhouse gases are released from burning coal and other fuels, which people need for power. The first, second, and third choices are facts, but don't show a relationship to the main idea.

5. A good concluding sentence might read: In conclusion, the best thing you can do for yourself is to skip the bestsellers and get your hands on some classics. This tells you how to go about finding the books in the paragraph.

6. D: This is the best choice because it takes a look at the idea that scientists are not in complete agreement about climate change. Choice A takes only one position, option B is more of a detail that may go in the essay, and choice C is about a different topic.

7. "For example" would be the best transition, because the sentences clearly show that an example of something is coming next.

8. C: "Green" products refer to those items that are safer for the environment and people than other conventional items.

9. B: This is the best choice because it mentions the main idea (issues the school faces) and provides an adequate summary of the topic.

10. B: The two men are talking about four possible dimensions and their ability to move through them.

11. The definition of spasmodic is occurring or done in brief, irregular bursts. Some good choices for synonyms would be "occasional" or "intermittent".

12. A: It is the only answer that correctly describes the two passages. Option B incorrectly identifies an explanation of gravity as the key point of interest in the passage from <u>The Time Machine</u>, option C incorrectly describes <u>The Time Machine</u> as being like the speech and vice versa, and option D incorrectly describes the concept of time travel as simple and the presentation of simple issues as inarguable.

13. C: It builds suspense because the Time Traveller already knows about the outcome of his experiments with time travel, and he is only leading his audience along by explaining the thought process behind it.

14. D: Electrical is the correct answer because the entire selection is about electricity and magnetism. Nothing in the article mentions molecular tools (A); and the other two answers, which come from the text, would not make sense in this context.

15. C: "Compress" is the word closest in meaning to the underlined word, "compact." While a compact can be a pledge or refer to something that is neat, efficient, or dense, these meanings cannot be derived from the context.

16. C: This would be the best way to help students see how the molecules move in metal. Then, a discussion afterwards would help to clarify any issues raised about the movie. The first choice only relies on text to explain this difficult concept, which may not be enough for most learners. Only asking discussion questions about magnetism would probably not help students if they did not already have a good idea of how magnetism worked, and seeing a representation of the electro-magnetic spectrum would not be able to explain how magnetism operates.

17. D: This is the best choice because it provides a simple description of how someone can see magnetism in his or her daily life.

18. Both of the speakers are arguing over the respect due to an individual, but they are going about it in different ways.

19. C: This detail would only really support the argument against wearing school uniforms, while the other three choices could all appear as details in support of either side of the argument.

20. A: The text indicates that the "rebel fire was hottest, the shells rolling down every street, and the bridge under the heavy cannonade" and "a courier... placed in my hand a crumpled, bloody piece of paper, a request from the lion-hearted old surgeon on the opposite shore, establishing his hospitals in the very jaws of death." Both of these indicate that the soldiers knew that the situation was dangerous, no place for an unarmed lady.

21. A: The text mentions Clara being helpful during several battles. While she may have helped throughout the Civil War, it is not the topic here. Choice C focuses more on other nurses in the war, and Choice D doesn't make sense because Clara was on the battlefield when the fighting was taking place.

22. C: The author mentions that men had been shot while Clara lived, demonstrating an interesting dichotomy of her life: the unarmed nurse who was protected on the battlefield, while the armed men did not seem to be.

23. B: While the other choices may have some truth to them, there is no evidence in the text that the soldier had little money (A). Options C and D give only partial answers.

24. D: Shakespeare uses a pun, or a play on words, to add character to the scene.

25. It is a noun. This is stated explicitly in the definition as "n" for noun.

26. B: This choice is the best because it establishes a consistent point of view, a tone, a period of time, and engages the reader with two questions: why M'ze hates work and why his mother is in the hospital.

27. D: A frame narrative uses a main story to tell either one or more stories inside of it. Frankenstein is a multiple frame story: the young man tells of Dr. Frankenstein, who in turn also tells the Monster's tale.

28. B: This is the only choice that makes sense. The sentences indicate that there may have been something that Darwin understood, a negative appears in the sentence (...Darwin did not have access...). The second sentence is obviously following a counting pattern (Secondly).

29. B: This answer comes directly from the text and the narrator's elaborate description of his father's grave and its location. Options A and D describe things that the passage does not describe as vividly, while option C makes reference to a mirror reflection that is not mentioned in the passage at all.

30. A: This is the only choice that mentions how the author feels about his father and follows the sadness and longing in the narrative. Choices A and B do not adequately show how the author feels towards his father and choice D refers to the supernatural, which is not mentioned here.

31. According to MLA format there should be a comma in between the last name and first, not a period. It should read: *Schwartz, Michael J. What's New Is Old. New York: Classic Books, 2012.*

32. B: My Antonia by Willa Cather is a classic tale about a woman's life in Nebraska with a strong theme of personal independence and self-respect.

33. B: The past participle usually goes along with "have" or "had."

34. C: The other choices all use the active voice. For sentences involving the passive voice, the subject of the sentence gets the action from the verb.

35. A: The other sentences either incorrectly use the comma (if at all) or the dash.

36. C: "Analysis" is the correct spelling of the word.

37. D: The emphasis on the actions of the listeners can be seen in the words "ask," "you," and "do."

38. A: While all of the words are similar in meaning, the passage refers to the people as "heroes" and the sorceress as "willowy," so the connotation of the word should be positive.

39. D: This is taken from Martin Luther King Jr.'s "I Have a Dream" speech in 1963. In it, King discussed important issues of race and equality while expressing his hope for the future.

40. C: This choice shows the appropriate mood and tense. The other examples show mixed constructions (A) and errors in the construction (B) or verb tense (D).

Success Strategies

The most important thing you can do is to ignore your fears and jump into the test immediately. Do not be overwhelmed by any strange-sounding terms. You have to jump into the test like jumping into a pool—all at once is the easiest way.

Make Predictions

As you read and understand the question, try to guess what the answer will be. Remember that several of the answer choices are wrong, and once you begin reading them, your mind will immediately become cluttered with answer choices designed to throw you off. Your mind is typically the most focused immediately after you have read the question and digested its contents. If you can, try to predict what the correct answer will be. You may be surprised at what you can predict.

Quickly scan the choices and see if your prediction is in the listed answer choices. If it is, then you can be quite confident that you have the right answer. It still won't hurt to check the other answer choices, but most of the time, you've got it!

Answer the Question

It may seem obvious to only pick answer choices that answer the question, but the test writers can create some excellent answer choices that are wrong. Don't pick an answer just because it sounds right, or you believe it to be true. It MUST answer the question. Once you've made your selection, always go back and check it against the question and make sure that you didn't misread the question and that the answer choice does answer the question posed.

Benchmark

After you read the first answer choice, decide if you think it sounds correct or not. If it doesn't, move on to the next answer choice. If it does, mentally mark that answer choice. This doesn't mean that you've definitely selected it as your answer choice, it just means that it's the best you've seen thus far. Go ahead and read the next choice. If the next choice is worse than the one you've already selected, keep going to the next answer choice. If the next choice is better than the choice you've already selected, mentally mark the new answer choice as your best guess.

The first answer choice that you select becomes your standard. Every other answer choice must be benchmarked against that standard. That choice is correct until proven otherwise by another answer choice beating it out. Once you've decided that no other answer choice seems as good, do one final check to ensure that your answer choice answers the question posed.

Valid Information

Don't discount any of the information provided in the question. Every piece of information may be necessary to determine the correct answer. None of the information in the question is there to throw you off (while the answer choices will certainly have information to throw you off). If two seemingly unrelated topics are discussed, don't ignore either. You can be confident there is a relationship, or it wouldn't be included in the question, and you are probably going to have to determine what is that relationship to find the answer.

Avoid "Fact Traps"

Don't get distracted by a choice that is factually true. Your search is for the answer that answers the question. Stay focused and don't fall for an answer that is true but irrelevant. Always go back to the question and make sure you're choosing an answer that actually answers the question and is not just a true statement. An answer can be factually correct, but it MUST answer the question asked. Additionally, two answers can both be seemingly correct, so be sure to read all of the answer choices, and make sure that you get the one that BEST answers the question.

Milk the Question

Some of the questions may throw you completely off. They might deal with a subject you have not been exposed to, or one that you haven't reviewed in years. While your lack of knowledge about the subject will be a hindrance, the question itself can give you many clues that will help you find the correct answer. Read the question carefully and look for clues. Watch particularly for adjectives and nouns describing difficult terms or words that you don't recognize. Regardless of whether you completely understand a word or not, replacing it with a synonym, either provided or one you more familiar with, may help you to understand what the questions are asking. Rather than wracking your mind about specific detailed information concerning a difficult term or word, try to use mental substitutes that are easier to understand.

The Trap of Familiarity

Don't just choose a word because you recognize it. On difficult questions, you may not recognize a number of words in the answer choices. The test writers don't put "make-believe" words on the test, so don't think that just because you only recognize all the words in one answer choice that that answer choice must be correct. If you only recognize words in one answer choice, then focus on that one. Is it correct? Try your best to determine if it is correct. If it is, that's great. If not, eliminate it. Each word and answer choice you eliminate increases your chances of getting the question correct, even if you then have to guess among the unfamiliar choices.

Eliminate Answers

Eliminate choices as soon as you realize they are wrong. But be careful! Make sure you consider all of the possible answer choices. Just because one appears right, doesn't mean that the next one won't be even better! The test writers will usually put more than one good answer choice for every question, so read all of them. Don't worry if you are stuck between two that seem right. By getting down to just two remaining possible choices, your odds are now 50/50. Rather than wasting too much time, play the odds. You are guessing, but guessing wisely because you've been able to knock out some of the answer choices that you know are wrong. If you are eliminating choices and realize that the last answer choice you are left with is also obviously wrong, don't panic. Start over and consider each choice again. There may easily be something that you missed the first time and will realize on the second pass.

Tough Questions

If you are stumped on a problem or it appears too hard or too difficult, don't waste time. Move on! Remember though, if you can quickly check for obviously incorrect answer choices, your chances of guessing correctly are greatly improved. Before you completely give up, at least try to knock out a couple of possible answers. Eliminate what you can and then guess at the remaining answer choices before moving on.

Brainstorm

If you get stuck on a difficult question, spend a few seconds quickly brainstorming. Run through the complete list of possible answer choices. Look at each choice and ask yourself, "Could this answer the question satisfactorily?" Go through each answer choice and consider it independently of the others. By systematically going through all possibilities, you may find something that you would otherwise overlook. Remember though that when you get stuck, it's important to try to keep moving.

Read Carefully

Understand the problem. Read the question and answer choices carefully. Don't miss the question because you misread the terms. You have plenty of time to read each question thoroughly and make sure you understand what is being asked. Yet a happy medium must be attained, so don't waste too much time. You must read carefully, but efficiently.

Face Value

When in doubt, use common sense. Always accept the situation in the problem at face value. Don't read too much into it. These problems will not require you to make huge leaps of logic. The test writers aren't trying to throw you off with a cheap trick. If you have to go beyond creativity and make a leap of logic in order to have an answer choice answer the question, then you should look at the other answer choices. Don't overcomplicate the problem by creating theoretical relationships or explanations that will warp time or space. These are normal problems rooted in reality. It's just that the applicable relationship or explanation may not be readily apparent and you have to figure things out. Use your common sense to interpret anything that isn't clear.

Prefixes

If you're having trouble with a word in the question or answer choices, try dissecting it. Take advantage of every clue that the word might include. Prefixes and suffixes can be a huge help. Usually they allow you to determine a basic meaning. Pre- means before, post- means after, pro - is positive, de- is negative. From these prefixes and suffixes, you can get an idea of the general meaning of the word and try to put it into context. Beware though of any traps. Just because con- is the opposite of pro-, doesn't necessarily mean congress is the opposite of progress!

Hedge Phrases

Watch out for critical hedge phrases, led off with words such as "likely," "may," "can," "sometimes," "often," "almost," "mostly," "usually," "generally," "rarely," and "sometimes." Question writers insert these hedge phrases to cover every possibility. Often an answer choice will be wrong simply because it leaves no room for exception. Unless the situation calls for them, avoid answer choices that have definitive words like "exactly," and "always."

Switchback Words

Stay alert for "switchbacks." These are the words and phrases frequently used to alert you to shifts in thought. The most common switchback word is "but." Others include "although," "however," "nevertheless," "on the other hand," "even though," "while," "in spite of," "despite," and "regardless of."

New Information

Correct answer choices will rarely have completely new information included. Answer choices typically are straightforward reflections of the material asked about and will directly relate to the question. If a new piece of information is included in an answer choice that doesn't even seem to relate to the topic being asked about, then that answer choice is likely incorrect. All of the information needed to answer the question is usually provided for you in the question. You should not have to make guesses that are unsupported or choose answer choices that require unknown information that cannot be reasoned from what is given.

Time Management

On technical questions, don't get lost on the technical terms. Don't spend too much time on any one question. If you don't know what a term means, then odds are you aren't going to get much further since you don't have a dictionary. You should be able to immediately recognize whether or not you know a term. If you don't, work with the other clues that you have—the other answer choices and terms provided—but don't waste too much time trying to figure out a difficult term that you don't know.

Contextual Clues

Look for contextual clues. An answer can be right but not the correct answer. The contextual clues will help you find the answer that is most right and is correct. Understand the context in which a phrase or statement is made. This will help you make important distinctions.

Don't Panic

Panicking will not answer any questions for you; therefore, it isn't helpful. When you first see the question, if your mind goes blank, take a deep breath. Force yourself to mechanically go through the steps of solving the problem using the strategies you've learned.

Pace Yourself

Don't get clock fever. It's easy to be overwhelmed when you're looking at a page full of questions, your mind is full of random thoughts and feeling confused, and the clock is ticking down faster than you would like. Calm down and maintain the pace that you have set for yourself. As long as you are on track by monitoring your pace, you are guaranteed to have enough time for yourself. When you get to the last few minutes of the test, it may seem like you won't have enough time left, but if you only have as many questions as you should have left at that point, then you're right on track!

Answer Selection

The best way to pick an answer choice is to eliminate all of those that are wrong, until only one is left and confirm that is the correct answer. Sometimes though, an answer choice may immediately look right. Be careful! Take a second to make sure that the other choices are not equally obvious. Don't make a hasty mistake. There are only two times that you should stop before checking other answers. First is when you are positive that the answer choice you have selected is correct. Second is when time is almost out and you have to make a quick guess!

Check Your Work

Since you will probably not know every term listed and the answer to every question, it is important that you get credit for the ones that you do know. Don't miss any questions through careless mistakes. If at all possible, try to take a second to look back over your answer selection and make sure you've selected the correct answer choice and haven't made a costly careless mistake (such as marking an answer choice that you didn't mean to mark). The time it takes for this quick double check should more than pay for itself in caught mistakes.

Beware of Directly Quoted Answers

Sometimes an answer choice will repeat word for word a portion of the question or reference section. However, beware of such exact duplication. It may be a trap! More than likely, the correct choice will paraphrase or summarize a point, rather than being exactly the same wording.

Slang

Scientific sounding answers are better than slang ones. An answer choice that begins "To compare the outcomes..." is much more likely to be correct than one that begins "Because some people insisted..."

Extreme Statements

Avoid wild answers that throw out highly controversial ideas that are proclaimed as established fact. An answer choice that states the "process should used in certain situations, if..." is much more likely to be correct than one that states the "process should be discontinued completely." The first is a calm rational statement and doesn't even make a definitive, uncompromising stance, using a hedge word "if" to provide wiggle room, whereas the second choice is a radical idea and far more extreme.

Answer Choice Families

When you have two or more answer choices that are direct opposites or parallels, one of them is usually the correct answer. For instance, if one answer choice states "x increases" and another answer choice states "x decreases" or "y increases," then those two or three answer choices are very similar in construction and fall into the same family of answer choices. A family of answer choices consists of two or three answer choices, very similar in construction, but often with directly opposite meanings. Usually the correct answer choice will be in that family of answer choices. The "odd man out" or answer choice that doesn't seem to fit the parallel construction of the other answer choices is more likely to be incorrect.

How to Overcome Test Anxiety

The very nature of tests caters to some level of anxiety, nervousness, or tension, just as we feel for any important event that occurs in our lives. A little bit of anxiety or nervousness can be a good thing. It helps us with motivation, and makes achievement just that much sweeter. However, too much anxiety can be a problem, especially if it hinders our ability to function and perform.

"Test anxiety," is the term that refers to the emotional reactions that some test-takers experience when faced with a test or exam. Having a fear of testing and exams is based upon a rational fear, since the test-taker's performance can shape the course of an academic career. Nevertheless, experiencing excessive fear of examinations will only interfere with the test-taker's ability to perform and chance to be successful.

There are a large variety of causes that can contribute to the development and sensation of test anxiety. These include, but are not limited to, lack of preparation and worrying about issues surrounding the test.

Lack of Preparation

Lack of preparation can be identified by the following behaviors or situations:
- Not scheduling enough time to study, and therefore cramming the night before the test or exam
- Managing time poorly, to create the sensation that there is not enough time to do everything
- Failing to organize the text information in advance, so that the study material consists of the entire text and not simply the pertinent information
- Poor overall studying habits

Worrying, on the other hand, can be related to both the test taker, or many other factors around him/her that will be affected by the results of the test. These include worrying about:
- Previous performances on similar exams, or exams in general
- How friends and other students are achieving
- The negative consequences that will result from a poor grade or failure

There are three primary elements to test anxiety. Physical components, which involve the same typical bodily reactions as those to acute anxiety (to be discussed below). Emotional factors have to do with fear or panic. Mental or cognitive issues concerning attention spans and memory abilities.

Physical Signals

There are many different symptoms of test anxiety, and these are not limited to mental and emotional strain. Frequently there are a range of physical signals that will let a test taker know that he/she is suffering from test anxiety. These bodily changes can include the following:

- Perspiring
- Sweaty palms
- Wet, trembling hands
- Nausea
- Dry mouth
- A knot in the stomach
- Headache
- Faintness
- Muscle tension
- Aching shoulders, back and neck
- Rapid heart beat
- Feeling too hot/cold

To recognize the sensation of test anxiety, a test-taker should monitor him/herself for the following sensations:

- The physical distress symptoms as listed above
- Emotional sensitivity, expressing emotional feelings such as the need to cry or laugh too much, or a sensation of anger or helplessness
- A decreased ability to think, causing the test-taker to blank out or have racing thoughts that are hard to organize or control.

Though most students will feel some level of anxiety when faced with a test or exam, the majority can cope with that anxiety and maintain it at a manageable level. However, those who cannot are faced with a very real and very serious condition, which can and should be controlled for the immeasurable benefit of this sufferer.

Naturally, these sensations lead to negative results for the testing experience. The most common effects of test anxiety have to do with nervousness and mental blocking.

Nervousness

Nervousness can appear in several different levels:

- The test-taker's difficulty, or even inability to read and understand the questions on the test
- The difficulty or inability to organize thoughts to a coherent form
- The difficulty or inability to recall key words and concepts relating to the testing questions (especially essays)
- The receipt of poor grades on a test, though the test material was well known by the test taker

Conversely, a person may also experience mental blocking, which involves:

- Blanking out on test questions
- Only remembering the correct answers to the questions when the test has already finished.

Fortunately for test anxiety sufferers, beating these feelings, to a large degree, has to do with proper preparation. When a test taker has a feeling of preparedness, then anxiety will be dramatically lessened.

The first step to resolving anxiety issues is to distinguish which of the two types of anxiety are being suffered. If the anxiety is a direct result of a lack of preparation, this should be considered a normal reaction, and the anxiety level (as opposed to the test results) shouldn't be anything to worry about. However, if, when adequately prepared, the test-taker still panics, blanks out, or seems to overreact, this is not a fully rational reaction. While this can be considered normal too, there are many ways to combat and overcome these effects.

Remember that anxiety cannot be entirely eliminated, however, there are ways to minimize it, to make the anxiety easier to manage. Preparation is one of the best ways to minimize test anxiety. Therefore the following techniques are wise in order to best fight off any anxiety that may want to build.

To begin with, try to avoid cramming before a test, whenever it is possible. By trying to memorize an entire term's worth of information in one day, you'll be shocking your system, and not giving yourself a very good chance to absorb the information. This is an easy path to anxiety, so for those who suffer from test anxiety, cramming should not even be considered an option.

Instead of cramming, work throughout the semester to combine all of the material which is presented throughout the semester, and work on it gradually as the course goes by, making sure to master the main concepts first, leaving minor details for a week or so before the test.

To study for the upcoming exam, be sure to pose questions that may be on the examination, to gauge the ability to answer them by integrating the ideas from your texts, notes and lectures, as well as any supplementary readings.

If it is truly impossible to cover all of the information that was covered in that particular term, concentrate on the most important portions, that can be covered very well. Learn these concepts as best as possible, so that when the test comes, a goal can be made to use these concepts as presentations of your knowledge.

In addition to study habits, changes in attitude are critical to beating a struggle with test anxiety. In fact, an improvement of the perspective over the entire test-taking experience can actually help a test taker to enjoy studying and therefore improve the overall experience. Be certain not to overemphasize the significance of the grade - know that the result of the test is neither a reflection of self worth, nor is it a measure of intelligence; one grade will not predict a person's future success.

To improve an overall testing outlook, the following steps should be tried:
- Keeping in mind that the most reasonable expectation for taking a test is to expect to try to demonstrate as much of what you know as you possibly can.
- Reminding ourselves that a test is only one test; this is not the only one, and there will be others.
- The thought of thinking of oneself in an irrational, all-or-nothing term should be avoided at all costs.

- A reward should be designated for after the test, so there's something to look forward to. Whether it be going to a movie, going out to eat, or simply visiting friends, schedule it in advance, and do it no matter what result is expected on the exam.

Test-takers should also keep in mind that the basics are some of the most important things, even beyond anti-anxiety techniques and studying. Never neglect the basic social, emotional and biological needs, in order to try to absorb information. In order to best achieve, these three factors must be held as just as important as the studying itself.

Study Steps

Remember the following important steps for studying:
- Maintain healthy nutrition and exercise habits. Continue both your recreational activities and social pass times. These both contribute to your physical and emotional well being.
- Be certain to get a good amount of sleep, especially the night before the test, because when you're overtired you are not able to perform to the best of your best ability.
- Keep the studying pace to a moderate level by taking breaks when they are needed, and varying the work whenever possible, to keep the mind fresh instead of getting bored.
- When enough studying has been done that all the material that can be learned has been learned, and the test taker is prepared for the test, stop studying and do something relaxing such as listening to music, watching a movie, or taking a warm bubble bath.

There are also many other techniques to minimize the uneasiness or apprehension that is experienced along with test anxiety before, during, or even after the examination. In fact, there are a great deal of things that can be done to stop anxiety from interfering with lifestyle and performance. Again, remember that anxiety will not be eliminated entirely, and it shouldn't be. Otherwise that "up" feeling for exams would not exist, and most of us depend on that sensation to perform better than usual. However, this anxiety has to be at a level that is manageable.

Of course, as we have just discussed, being prepared for the exam is half the battle right away. Attending all classes, finding out what knowledge will be expected on the exam, and knowing the exam schedules are easy steps to lowering anxiety. Keeping up with work will remove the need to cram, and efficient study habits will eliminate wasted time. Studying should be done in an ideal location for concentration, so that it is simple to become interested in the material and give it complete attention. A method such as SQ3R (Survey, Question, Read, Recite, Review) is a wonderful key to follow to make sure that the study habits are as effective as possible, especially in the case of learning from a textbook. Flashcards are great techniques for memorization. Learning to take good notes will mean that notes will be full of useful information, so that less sifting will need to be done to seek out what is pertinent for studying. Reviewing notes after class and then again on occasion will keep the information fresh in the mind. From notes that have been taken summary sheets and outlines can be made for simpler reviewing.

A study group can also be a very motivational and helpful place to study, as there will be a sharing of ideas, all of the minds can work together, to make sure that everyone understands, and the studying will be made more interesting because it will be a social occasion.

Basically, though, as long as the test-taker remains organized and self confident, with efficient study habits, less time will need to be spent studying, and higher grades will be achieved.

To become self confident, there are many useful steps. The first of these is "self talk." It has been shown through extensive research, that self-talk for students who suffer from test anxiety, should be well monitored, in order to make sure that it contributes to self confidence as opposed to sinking the student. Frequently the self talk of test-anxious students is negative or self-defeating, thinking that everyone else is smarter and faster, that they always mess up, and that if they don't do well, they'll fail the entire course. It is important to decreasing anxiety that awareness is made of self talk. Try writing any negative self thoughts and then disputing them with a positive statement instead. Begin self-encouragement as though it was a friend speaking. Repeat positive statements to help reprogram the mind to believing in successes instead of failures.

Helpful Techniques

Other extremely helpful techniques include:
- Self-visualization of doing well and reaching goals
- While aiming for an "A" level of understanding, don't try to "overprotect" by setting your expectations lower. This will only convince the mind to stop studying in order to meet the lower expectations.
- Don't make comparisons with the results or habits of other students. These are individual factors, and different things work for different people, causing different results.
- Strive to become an expert in learning what works well, and what can be done in order to improve. Consider collecting this data in a journal.
- Create rewards for after studying instead of doing things before studying that will only turn into avoidance behaviors.
- Make a practice of relaxing - by using methods such as progressive relaxation, self-hypnosis, guided imagery, etc - in order to make relaxation an automatic sensation.
- Work on creating a state of relaxed concentration so that concentrating will take on the focus of the mind, so that none will be wasted on worrying.
- Take good care of the physical self by eating well and getting enough sleep.
- Plan in time for exercise and stick to this plan.

Beyond these techniques, there are other methods to be used before, during and after the test that will help the test-taker perform well in addition to overcoming anxiety.

Before the exam comes the academic preparation. This involves establishing a study schedule and beginning at least one week before the actual date of the test. By doing this, the anxiety of not having enough time to study for the test will be automatically eliminated.

Moreover, this will make the studying a much more effective experience, ensuring that the learning will be an easier process. This relieves much undue pressure on the test-taker.

Summary sheets, note cards, and flash cards with the main concepts and examples of these main concepts should be prepared in advance of the actual studying time. A topic should never be eliminated from this process. By omitting a topic because it isn't expected to be on the test is only setting up the test-taker for anxiety should it actually appear on the exam. Utilize the course syllabus for laying out the topics that should be studied. Carefully go over the notes that were made in class, paying special attention to any of the issues that the professor took special care to emphasize while lecturing in class. In the textbooks, use the chapter review, or if possible, the chapter tests, to begin your review.

It may even be possible to ask the instructor what information will be covered on the exam, or what the format of the exam will be (for example, multiple choice, essay, free form, true-false). Additionally, see if it is possible to find out how many questions will be on the test. If a review sheet or sample test has been offered by the professor, make good use of it, above anything else, for the preparation for the test. Another great resource for getting to know the examination is reviewing tests from previous semesters. Use these tests to review, and aim to achieve a 100% score on each of the possible topics. With a few exceptions, the goal that you set for yourself is the highest one that you will reach.

Take all of the questions that were assigned as homework, and rework them to any other possible course material. The more problems reworked, the more skill and confidence will form as a result. When forming the solution to a problem, write out each of the steps. Don't simply do head work. By doing as many steps on paper as possible, much clarification and therefore confidence will be formed. Do this with as many homework problems as possible, before checking the answers. By checking the answer after each problem, a reinforcement will exist, that will not be on the exam. Study situations should be as exam-like as possible, to prime the test-taker's system for the experience. By waiting to check the answers at the end, a psychological advantage will be formed, to decrease the stress factor.

Another fantastic reason for not cramming is the avoidance of confusion in concepts, especially when it comes to mathematics. 8-10 hours of study will become one hundred percent more effective if it is spread out over a week or at least several days, instead of doing it all in one sitting. Recognize that the human brain requires time in order to assimilate new material, so frequent breaks and a span of study time over several days will be much more beneficial.

Additionally, don't study right up until the point of the exam. Studying should stop a minimum of one hour before the exam begins. This allows the brain to rest and put things in their proper order. This will also provide the time to become as relaxed as possible when going into the examination room. The test-taker will also have time to eat well and eat sensibly. Know that the brain needs food as much as the rest of the body. With enough food and enough sleep, as well as a relaxed attitude, the body and the mind are primed for success.

Avoid any anxious classmates who are talking about the exam. These students only spread anxiety, and are not worth sharing the anxious sentimentalities.

Before the test also involves creating a positive attitude, so mental preparation should also be a point of concentration. There are many keys to creating a positive attitude. Should fears become rushing in, make a visualization of taking the exam, doing well, and seeing an A written on the paper. Write out a list of affirmations that will bring a feeling of confidence, such as "I am doing well in my English class," "I studied well and know my material," "I enjoy this class." Even if the affirmations aren't believed at first, it sends a positive message to the subconscious which will result in an alteration of the overall belief system, which is the system that creates reality.

If a sensation of panic begins, work with the fear and imagine the very worst! Work through the entire scenario of not passing the test, failing the entire course, and dropping out of school, followed by not getting a job, and pushing a shopping cart through the dark alley where you'll live. This will place things into perspective! Then, practice deep breathing and create a visualization of the opposite situation - achieving an "A" on the exam, passing the entire course, receiving the degree at a graduation ceremony.

On the day of the test, there are many things to be done to ensure the best results, as well as the most calm outlook. The following stages are suggested in order to maximize test-taking potential:

- Begin the examination day with a moderate breakfast, and avoid any coffee or beverages with caffeine if the test taker is prone to jitters. Even people who are used to managing caffeine can feel jittery or light-headed when it is taken on a test day.
- Attempt to do something that is relaxing before the examination begins. As last minute cramming clouds the mastering of overall concepts, it is better to use this time to create a calming outlook.
- Be certain to arrive at the test location well in advance, in order to provide time to select a location that is away from doors, windows and other distractions, as well as giving enough time to relax before the test begins.
- Keep away from anxiety generating classmates who will upset the sensation of stability and relaxation that is being attempted before the exam.
- Should the waiting period before the exam begins cause anxiety, create a self-distraction by reading a light magazine or something else that is relaxing and simple.

During the exam itself, read the entire exam from beginning to end, and find out how much time should be allotted to each individual problem. Once writing the exam, should more time be taken for a problem, it should be abandoned, in order to begin another problem. If there is time at the end, the unfinished problem can always be returned to and completed.

Read the instructions very carefully - twice - so that unpleasant surprises won't follow during or after the exam has ended.

When writing the exam, pretend that the situation is actually simply the completion of homework within a library, or at home. This will assist in forming a relaxed atmosphere, and will allow the brain extra focus for the complex thinking function.

Begin the exam with all of the questions with which the most confidence is felt. This will build the confidence level regarding the entire exam and will begin a quality momentum. This will also create encouragement for trying the problems where uncertainty resides.

Going with the "gut instinct" is always the way to go when solving a problem. Second guessing should be avoided at all costs. Have confidence in the ability to do well.

For essay questions, create an outline in advance that will keep the mind organized and make certain that all of the points are remembered. For multiple choice, read every answer, even if the correct one has been spotted - a better one may exist.

Continue at a pace that is reasonable and not rushed, in order to be able to work carefully. Provide enough time to go over the answers at the end, to check for small errors that can be corrected.

Should a feeling of panic begin, breathe deeply, and think of the feeling of the body releasing sand through its pores. Visualize a calm, peaceful place, and include all of the sights, sounds and sensations of this image. Continue the deep breathing, and take a few minutes to continue this with closed eyes. When all is well again, return to the test.

If a "blanking" occurs for a certain question, skip it and move on to the next question. There will be time to return to the other question later. Get everything done that can be done, first, to guarantee all the grades that can be compiled, and to build all of the confidence possible. Then return to the weaker questions to build the marks from there.

Remember, one's own reality can be created, so as long as the belief is there, success will follow. And remember: anxiety can happen later, right now, there's an exam to be written!

After the examination is complete, whether there is a feeling for a good grade or a bad grade, don't dwell on the exam, and be certain to follow through on the reward that was promised...and enjoy it! Don't dwell on any mistakes that have been made, as there is nothing that can be done at this point anyway.

Additionally, don't begin to study for the next test right away. Do something relaxing for a while, and let the mind relax and prepare itself to begin absorbing information again.

From the results of the exam - both the grade and the entire experience, be certain to learn from what has gone on. Perfect studying habits and work some more on confidence in order to make the next examination experience even better than the last one.

Learn to avoid places where openings occurred for laziness, procrastination and day dreaming.

Use the time between this exam and the next one to better learn to relax, even learning to relax on cue, so that any anxiety can be controlled during the next exam. Learn how to relax the body. Slouch in your chair if that helps. Tighten and then relax all of the different muscle groups, one group at a time, beginning with the feet and then working all the way up to the neck and face. This will ultimately relax the muscles more than they were to begin with. Learn how to breathe deeply and comfortably, and focus on this breathing going in and out as a relaxing thought. With every exhale, repeat the word "relax."

As common as test anxiety is, it is very possible to overcome it. Make yourself one of the test-takers who overcome this frustrating hindrance.

Additional Bonus Material

Due to our efforts to try to keep this book to a manageable length, we've created a link that will give you access to all of your additional bonus material.

Please visit http://www.mometrix.com/bonus948/terrag8 to access the information.